Audiences

a teacher's guide

Roger Martin

Auteur

Roger Martin

is Head of Media and Film Studies at Godalming College.

First Published 2004

by Auteur

The Old Surgery, 9 Pulford Road, Leighton Buzzard, Bedfordshire LU7 1AB

© Auteur Publishing, 2004

ISBN 1-903663-18-0

Auteur on the internet: http://www.auteur.co.uk

Designed and typeset by Loaf, PO Box 737, Cottenham, Cambridge CB4 8BA

Printed by The Direct Printing Company, Brixworth, Northamptonshire

Contents

Introduction

The 'audience' has become a volatile battleground within the media industries and a controversial concept within media and cultural studies. Politicians, academics, parents and educationists, have all weighed into the debate on such issues as cultural 'dumbing down' and the allegedly pernicious effects of television violence. Certainties about the nature of the audience seem to have been eroded in inverse proportion to advances made in the technology of measurement. It has even been argued that, in any meaningful way, 'audience' exists only as a discursive entity, an epistemological fiction necessary for the maintenance of broadcasting economies. Be that as it may, real people actually do watch television and listen to the radio, real audiences do exist. The question remains, however – how are we to conceptualise 'audience'?

The word 'audience' has traditionally been used to refer to a group of people gathered together to watch and listen to some kind of public performance or address. The notion of audience with which we are familiar today existed in classical Greece and Rome. Denis McQuail (1997, p. 15) characterises this audience as follows:

- planning and *organisation* of viewing and listening, as well as of the performances themselves;

- events with a *public* and 'popular' character;

- secular (thus not religious) content of performance – for entertainment, education, and vicarious emotional experience;

- voluntary, individual acts of choice and attention;

- specialisation of roles, authors, performers and spectators;

- a specific physical location where a performance is attended by an audience.

The distinctive feature of such an audience is that its members are all in the same place at the same time, watching/viewing the same thing, albeit constructing different interpretations. But this notion of 'audience' has been radically transformed by the mass media. The traditional audience does still exist (in the theatre, for example), but the television and radio audience is significantly different. It is fragmented and situated in innumerable physical locations. It is also temporally fragmented: any one programme will be watched or listened to at different times, either because of time-shifting with any increasing range of recorders or through varied patterns of scheduling by broadcasters. Radio, television and films can also be accessed from the Internet, from anywhere in the world, at any time of day or night.

The quest to understand the audience has been pursued at different levels. There is the desire to understand what happens when a reader/spectator engages with a text: how do audiences make sense of what they see and hear? What are the conditions of meaning? There are long standing concerns about the effects of the media: in what ways do they influence behaviour? In commerce there is, of course, a financial imperative associated with behaviour modification. The need of the advertiser is to reach as large an audience as possible in the hope of increasing sales. It is with advertising that audience research largely began.

This *Teacher's Guide* begins with a brief overview of the history of audience research, outlining some of the issues dealt with more thoroughly later in the book. This is followed by more detailed accounts of the major theoretical approaches to *audience studies*: effects, uses and gratification and ethnological/reception research. This is followed by an overview of how audience research is done for television, radio and cinema and concludes with a consideration of recent developments in reception studies of fans. Finally, there is an account of reality TV, which by its very nature conflates issues of technology and the construction of the audience. The aim of the Guide is to provide a comprehensive guide to both the theory and practice of audience research that will serve the needs of teachers and students of Film and Media Studies.

Early Investigations

Will Brooker argues that the 'first transitional moment in the twentieth century in terms of the rise of audience studies' was World War I (Brooker 2003, p. 5) with the widespread use of the mass media for propaganda purposes. Propaganda had always been a feature of warfare, but in WWI it reached unprecedented levels of intensity. In the 1920s this led to both a concern and interest in the potential of the mass media for manipulating and controlling minds for both political and commercial purposes. The image of a passive audience that this implies, became part of the way in which society was characterised by the emerging 'mass society' thesis, which was supported by both the left and right in the 1930s. It seemed to be confirmed by the rise of Hitler and the Nazi Party and their use of the mass media. On the left of the political spectrum, the Frankfurt School (T.W. Adorno et al.) argued that culture was imposed from above onto a malleable and impressionable audience. Furthermore, the emerging 'mass culture industries', in particular Hollywood and advertising, threatened the values of this culture.

When broadcasting began in the 1920s, the USA, unlike the UK, opted for a free market system funded by advertising and sponsorship. It was not long before broadcasters and advertisers felt the need to investigate the efficacy of advertising and sponsorship. To begin with audience research was no more than a fairly primitive 'head count' achieved by requesting listeners to send a postcard if they were listening to the programme.

In fact John Grierson, who played such a seminal role in the creation of the British documentary movement, only became interested in film when his research in the American press faltered and it was suggested to him that he looked at Hollywood as an alternative. That was in 1928.

Audience research began at the BBC more or less the same way (Silvey 1974). Academic interest in the media was focused on the press and cinema.

In 1930, the first major enquiry into the effects of cinema on children (The Payne Report) was published in the USA. As to whether or not cinema had a negative influence on children, it was equivocal: a sign of things to come with television audience research.

Effects theory characterised the relationship between audience and media as one of subordination. The assumption was that responses were predictable, measurable and directly related to a specific media stimulus – a notion that was reassuring to politicians and advertisers alike. It became known as the '**hypodermic needle**' model, based upon the behaviourist idea of stimulus–response. However, whilst this might have worked with Pavlov's dogs, it was inadequate when it came to accounting for the complex emotional and thought processes that occur when an audience engages with a text.

A significant shift occurred in the 1940s, eventually leading to the effects approach being turned on its head. The shortcomings of the effects model were demonstrated by Paul Lazarsfeld et al.'s *The People's Choice: How the Voter Makes Up His Mind in a Presidential Campaign.* This was a study of the role of the media in the 1940 presidential campaign in which 600 people were questioned over the seven months prior to the election. The results, at the time, were surprising. The role of the media was found to be small and the direct link between media-message and behaviour was missing. In the third edition of the study, published in 1968, Lazarsfeld commented on a finding that had subsequently emerged from the research. It was found that what was significant in the formation of opinion was 'a great deal of person-to-person interaction'. The research produced evidence of the role of a group of articulate individuals who functioned as 'opinion leaders': their influence, and the general interaction of group members, was far more important in the formation of opinion than the mass media. This conclusion formed the basis of the 'two step flow' theory, i.e., that opinion is formed not 'top down' (the media down to the individual) but rather 'bottom up', through the intercession of the 'opinion leaders'. Lazarsfeld argued that opinion leaders themselves do not necessarily operate vertically, but also 'horizontally: there are opinion leaders in every walk of life' (1968, p.7). *The People's Choice* brought into question the ability of the media to directly influence opinion and behaviour, and as such undermined the central tenet of effects studies. However, as with all audience research, it raised questions, such as how much can validly be extrapolated from what was a very particular study of audience responses and then applied to audiences in general.

'**Uses and gratification**' shifted the focus from what the media did to the audience, to what the audience did with the media. The audience was conceived as being active interpreter-users, rather than passive recipients of mass media messages. A study undertaken by Katz, Gurevitch and Haas (1974) concluded that audiences discriminate among the media, looking for content that conforms to their psychological and social needs. This conclusion highlighted both the strength and weakness of uses and gratification theory insofar as it shifted (even more than Lazarsfeld had done) the emphasis towards the audience; but at the same time it provided a limited notion of media choice and use.

That audiences vary in their responses to the media was the subject of research undertaken at the University of Birmingham Centre for Contemporary Cultural Studies in the 1970s. A seminal paper was Stuart Hall's 1974 *Coding and Encoding in the Television Discourse*, subsequently used by David Morley in his *Nationwide* research. This proposed that audiences' readings are determined by their gender, social and ideological positions. Messages are encoded with a preferred reading, but audiences may well have different and alternative interpretations.

Morley's work marked a shift towards an **ethnological approach** to audience studies. These have been many and varied from the tentative steps towards working with 'real' audiences undertaken by Morley, to the participant-observer studies undertaken by Henry Jenkins. The potential weaknesses of this kind of work are clear, but perhaps no more disabling than those that come with any other approach to audience research. With much ethnographic research there are two layers of interpretation: there is the respondent's own memory, selection and construction of their responses, which in turn is then interpreted by the researcher. But such difficulties do not invalidate this work.

The ethnographical approach to reader response studies was pioneered by Janice Radway in her 1984 study of women's pleasure in reading romance fiction (*Reading the Romance: Women, Patriarchy and Popular Literature*). This study distanced itself from traditional academic literary studies in two ways: it took as its object of study a generally denigrated popular literary form, and employed research methods that were closer to anthropology than literary analysis. Radway argued that, for the women she worked with, what was read was as significant as how and why it was read. The act of reading itself was crucial in defining a personal space, separated from both the world of work and domestic responsibilities. Radway, in her introduction to the 1991 edition of *Reading the Romance*, highlighted a difficulty that is attendant upon much ethnographic work and that is the mediating influence she exerted in constructing the community of readers that she analysed. Radway rightly advocates a 'multifaceted approach' to audience studies embracing both ethnography and textual analysis.

The 'third generation' of ethnographic audience studies has focused on groups of fans. The work of Henry Jenkins, for example, has looked at *Star Trek* fans as an active interpretative community that uses the programme for a range of extra-textual activities that serve to reaffirm group and individual identities while enabling the fan audience to creatively appropriate the text and make it their own, to the point of challenging Paramount over issues of gay representation. Other studies with an ethnographic element include Ang's work on *Dallas* and its audiences and Henry Jenkins' work on *Star Trek* fans (see chapters one and five, respectively).

Audience Research

Forms of Research

Audience Research

There are two forms of research: **applied** and **theoretical**. Applied research tends to be carried out by, or on behalf of, commercial broadcasters and publishers: it 'is designed to supply practical information that can guide decision-making' (Webster et al. 2000, p. 1). The information needed is both the size of the audience and its demographic profile, including social class, age and gender. Theoretical research has tended to be undertaken by academic bodies. Some of the questions posed by this kind of research either have no immediate commercial 'pay off' or may even be inimical to commercial interests, insofar as there is a good deal of research that sets out to show that television is 'bad for you', in terms of it's alleged negative influence on behaviour and even, as some critics have argued, on the culture itself. Typical of the sort of questions posed by this kind of research are:

- effects of watching violence on television,
- why people use the media,
- explanations of how mass audiences are formed.

(Webster et al. p. 3)

Commercial (applied) audience research, so long yoked primarily to measurement, no longer diverts so radically from academic research. This is in part because of the continuing fragmenting of the television market through

A linked development is interactive media. To date, this does not seem to have gone much further than enabling the audience to 'press the red' button and vote. It is, however, through technological developments such as TiVo in the US and Sky Plus in the UK, some factual programmes, such as **Walking with Cavemen** (BBC, 2003) utilise an interactive element to provide audiences with supplementary information. Interactive television is likely to develop and incorporate elements of audience research: it is early days yet.

the expansion of cable, satellite and digital broadcasting and the concomitant increase in niche channels and programming: broadcasters need to know more about their audiences.

Whether it is applied or theoretical research, the first question is, what is being researched? The kinds of research questions that applied research attempts to answer can be summarised as follows:

1. Print (magazines and newspapers):
• the degree of recall on whether people remember seeing an advert;

• copy testing to assess the appeal/in formativeness of messages;

• the study of characteristics of people who read various publications.

2. Electronic Media:
• surveys to assess appeal of celebrities and popular music;

• auditorium testing to evaluate pilot programmes;

• ratings research to measure size and composition of audiences.

The audience is easier to measure in some media than others. Cinema and theatre audiences not only have a clear physical presence, but they are also relatively easy to measure through box office takings. With print media, although the number of readers is difficult to determine with any accuracy, there is at least a reliable base line which is the number that are sold. It is reasonable to assume that virtually all newspapers and magazines sold are read by at least one person, in fact the press work by the 'thumb rule' of three readers to every copy. But what of television? There are no box office receipts and neither is there anything tangible bought and sold. How then is the television audience to be measured? The essential problem is well known: because a television is switched on, it does not mean that the audience is – the TV might be playing to an empty room. Even if there is a notional audience, that is to say people present in front of the set, it does not mean that they are actually watching it. The audience may be distracted by some other activity. This presents commercial broadcasters with the problem of finding ways of accurately measuring not only the size of the audience, but also its demographic characteristics and patterns of behaviour. All of this data is important for both commercial and public broadcasters: the former need to know that the audience is responding positively to advertisements, while public broadcasters need to be satisfied that they are fulfilling their responsibilities to the audience maintaining a sufficiently large share of it to justify public funding.

Methodologies

Quantitative vs. Qualitative Research

More or less corresponding to the two types of audience research, are two methodologies: **quantitative** and **qualitative**. 'Quantitative' research is concerned with measurable data, and findings tend to be expressed statistically. Qualitative research, on the other hand, is less concerned with statistical data and more with in depth knowledge of, for example, opinion and behaviour patterns. Qualitative research tends to be based on interviews and observation. Usually, both forms of research go hand-in-hand, as they complement each other. Quantitative research has a broad reach and accumulates a lot of data. Figures such as ratings are good at indicating the exposure of a programme or advertisement, but will say nothing about what the audience thought of them. Qualitative research is good at providing that kind of information, as it is based on personal interviews, diaries, letters and so forth. However, qualitative research often lacks the credibility derived from a large-scale research project with its attendant empirical data. Research carried out by BARB, for example, utilises both types of research: as well as providing ratings that estimate the size of an audience for any given programme, they also provide an appreciation index, based on diaries and interviews.

Both kinds of research are carried out by specialist organisations such as BARB in the UK and Nielsen and Arbitron in the USA. Such companies produce a variety of research products, most of them generating standard data required by subscribing broadcasters, advertisers and other clients. This is *syndicated* research. Custom research is produced to fulfil a specific research need for an individual client. An advantage of syndicated research is that it is cheaper, as costs are spread out over a number of clients. Custom research is 'tailored to meet the needs of a particular sponsor and may never be seen by outsiders' (Webster et al. 2000, p. 5). Although mostly quantitative, there will be the occasional need for more theoretical, academic research, concerned with aggregates and not any individual audience member.

Most audience research is commercial, being directed at measuring audiences rather than studying 'the process through which the audiences reject or inject the information presented to them' (Bogart 1996, p. 138). The 'number crunching' emphasis of most commercial research does little to further understanding of how audiences make sense of what they see or how they use it. This type of research tends to:

• tell us little about why people use mass media;

• not explain the consequences of media use;

• reduce people to numerical summaries

• be skewed in favour of the client's needs as research is a commercial product that needs to be sold.

These concerns should be at the centre of any enquiry into audiences, but much commercial research is not designed to answer them. Every type of research has its limitations and there is a need to both identify and factor them into any research programme.

Methodological Research

Another type of applied research is **methodological** research, which is essentially research *about* research. The history of audience research, especially in television, is mapped out with attempts to maximise the accuracy and scope of audience measurement techniques. Television and radio audiences are notoriously difficult to 'capture' in terms of the empirical data required by broadcasters and advertisers. Even information as basic as the number of people watching or listening has been difficult to determine. Because of this, research into methodology and measuring technology has been of great importance to the broadcasting and advertising industries; research companies such as Arbitron and Nielsen achieved prominence by developing research methods that, each in turn, seemed to hold out the promise of greater accuracy. Arbitron and Nielsen 'sell a research product and like any business engage in product testing and development' (Webster et al. p. 2). Methodological research will include such questions as 'can we measure TV viewing more accurately?' or 'how can we improve the response rate to our surveys?' or 'can we design a better questionnaire?'

Applied and theoretical research are not mutually exclusive in terms of purpose. The methods of applied research are sometimes used by academics and theoretical research is sometimes used for commercial purposes. Paul Lazarsfeld made a distinction between administrative and critical studies (Lazarsfeld and Stanton 1941). Administrative studies are those undertaken in order to improve the operational effectiveness of an institution or procedure, such as determining the size of a television audience or the kind of audience it is, with its likes, dislikes and spending habits. Critical studies are more 'self consciously ideological' (Webster et al. 2000, p. 3) and engage with issues such as the effects of violence on behaviour, gender representation and the reinforcement (or otherwise) of stereotypes.

The Effects Tradition

Effects studies embrace both commercial and theoretical research paradigms. 'Effects studies' is an 'umbrella' term, embracing a variety of theoretical and empirical approaches. Effects studies began with the emergence of radio as a major advertising medium. Quite simply, advertisers needed to know how effective they were in appealing to audiences. However, what at times has seemed the single preoccupation of effects studies is the representation of violence and its effects on audiences, especially young audiences.

There does not seem to have been a time when there was not concern about the effects of 'media' texts. Plato banned poetry from his hypothetical republic, because he believed it would undermine the morality of its citizens. Later, in the Middle Ages, the Church was in fear of the printing press, because of the perceived danger that ordinary people would come to read the Bible and make their own interpretations of it. Since then, virtually each generation has been apprehensive of the real or imagined effects of each new media form that has appeared. There were concerns about the social effects of radio when the BBC first came on air in 1922. In the 1930s, in America, the Payne report on film and children highlighted the potential harmful effects of cinema on young minds; in the 1950s it was the turn of horror comics and television. Television remains a concern, now supplemented by video and computer games. The worry is that all of these media, in some way, wield a detrimental effect on social behaviour, especially with regard to violence. The inducement of violent behaviour or the acceptance of violence, has been the enduring charge laid at television and film. There have been other alleged effects. Television became the scapegoat for America's defeat by North Vietnam. It was long believed (and in some quarters still is) that exposure to brutal TV images gradually eroded the American public's will to prosecute the war.

Frankfurt School

An early attempt to understand 'effects' in terms of their ideological influence, rather than behavioural, ran parallel with the development of effects studies in the 1930s and 40s. The 'Frankfurt School' were a group of philosophers, sociologists and economists who were associated with the Institut für Sozialforschung (Institute for Social Research), an independently endowed foundation within the University of Frankfurt. The leading figures in this group were Horkheimer (from 1930 the Institute's Director), Habermas, Adorno, Marcuse, and, with a more problematic relationship with the institute, but an important contributor, Walter Benjamin (his work was posthumously edited by Adorno).

The rise of the Nazi Party in the 1930s caused many of the leading members of the Institute to flee the country, first to Switzerland and then America where the Institute for Social Research was established. As a group the Frankfurt School were hostile to the 'culture industry' and mass produced popular culture; they regarded themselves as defenders of an intellectual humanist tradition, grounded in modernism, that was threatened first by the rise of Fascism and then by an industrialised popular culture fed by Hollywood. The Frankfurt School was austerely intellectual and had a deeply pessimistic view of modern society. This was reflected in a later work entitled *The Authoritarian Personality* (Adorno et al. 1950). Influenced by Erich Fromm and Wilhelm Reich it posited the 'F-Scale' as a means of measuring the pre-Fascist tendencies of individuals with authoritarian personality traits.

McQuail, Blumler and
Brown (1972) formulated
a lexicon of 'uses'
(ROGER – need the
reference here):

*• Diversion/catharsis:
usually thought of as
'escapism', this is a
commonly accepted
function of fiction in all
its forms whether on
screen, radio, print,
stage – or game consul.
Aristotle identifies the
role of catharsis in his
Poetics (Dorsch, 1965)
(as bringing about the
release ('purging') of
emotions, thus reducing
them. Similar arguments
have been put forward
regarding screen
violence and
pornography.*

*• Personal relationships:
the media – especially
radio and television – can
be the source of
surrogate relationships.
The degree to which this
is the case range from
the psychotic, where the
imagined relationship
with a screen personality
is believed to be real, to
the much weaker
'attachment' we
probably all occasionally
feel towards media
personalities (presenters
and so on) and fictional
characters in drama, etc.*

*• Personal identity:
fiction in all its forms
provides a means by
which personal identity
can be reinforced and
value systems both
challenged and*

The Hypodermic Model

Effects studies have dominated the research on the influence
of media upon audiences, ranging from the efficacy of
advertising to the impact of screen violence on behaviour.
Although effects studies are not homogeneous, they tend
to be predicated upon a relatively simple communication
model. Essentially, the model is one of direct
communication, reduced to three elements, sender –
medium – receiver. This model has frequently been used
in association with behaviourist psychology: early versions
were based upon a kind of Pavlovian stimulus–response in
which the recipients were seen to behave in a way
appropriate to the content and form of the message. The
media 'injects' its message and the audience responds
accordingly. Appropriately enough, this has been called the
'hypodermic' or 'magic bullet' model. The audience is
constructed as a passive recipient, without the power to
determine the meaning of the message with which it has
been 'injected'. Effects studies have become more complex
and diverse, based upon more elaborate communication
models that incorporate 'intervening variables' – or 'noise'
– that in some way change the message. One irony is
that although this led to a change in the perception of
the power of the media (it increasingly came to be seen
not to wield the degree influence that was earlier
thought to be the case), it has not altered the perception
of the relationship between screen violence and
aggressive behaviour in individuals: the media, especially
television, is still seen to be a powerful influence.

Not withstanding the thousands of effects studies that
have been undertaken, there is still no clear
understanding of how the media influences audiences;
however, the claim made by effects studies is that there
is a direct correlation between the content of a message
and audience behaviour. Effects studies can be
characterised as:

• assuming the audience is passive;

• treating children as inadequate and in need of
protection;

- artificial, as research is frequently through lab experiments;
- failing to account for meaning of violence as portrayed on film/TV;
- regarding society as a collection of 'atomised' individuals;
- being selective in their criticisms of media depictions of violence;
- assuming superiority over audiences;
- not being grounded in theory.

conformed through, for example, drama.

• *Surveillance: the media are a prime source of information about the world. If these are sources of 'hard' information about the world, fiction can be a source of a range of cultural knowledge.*

Uses and Gratification: An Early Challenge

By the 1940s a mutated version of effects studies had turned the erstwhile perceived relationship between audience and media on its head. Effects studies tended to be about the media and the message: what became known as 'uses and gratification' emphasised the audience. The stress shifted from the idea of the passive to the active audience. This 'new' audience put the media to its own use in order to satisfy a range of psychological and social needs. The audience itself became the object of study as well as the media. There was also a shift towards seeing the audience as an interactive group, rather than focusing on the individual. The change in approach was neatly summed up John Halloran (1970): 'We must get away from the habit of thinking in terms of what the media do to people and substitute for it the idea of what people do with the media'.

Uses and gratifications approaches were an advance on effects studies. A 'uses and gratification' approach differs from most effects studies in the following ways:

- emphasises the role of the audience as *active* users of media products;
- takes into account the different *uses* people make of the media;

• tends to be phenomenological: in the approach to research people are asked about their media use.

Limitations

This approach has, however, been criticised on a number of accounts, in particular the relationship between 'uses' and 'gratification'. On the one hand, while there is an acknowledgement that individuals are the product of specific social circumstances, there is frequently a lack of any analysis of them. Graham Murdock, Phillip Elliott and others have argued that 'needs' ought to be understood within the context of the structural positions people occupy within society. Murdock also argues that media texts are not as open as is suggested by the 'uses and gratification' approach, that it underestimates the 'importance of ideological codes which "prefer" and promote particular ranges of meaning, signification and gratification over others' (Hartley et al. 1985).

Contexts/Consumption

Stuart Hall: Encoding/decoding

Murdock's own work is an attempt to investigate the ideological determinants on the way a text is read. His was one of five research projects published in the 1980s that developed a critical method proposed by Stuart Hall in *Encoding and Decoding in the Television Discourse* (1974). Hall was the first of three generations of academics who applied reception theory to television, followed by a series of studies that adopted an **ethnological approach**: Morley, Ang, Hobson, Katz and Liebes. All of these were qualitative reception studies of a single text. and its reception by a particular audience. After Morley, they became increasingly concerned with feminist issues. As a group of studies, they 'started to look at the audiences', studying how the programme related to their lives of the respondents. Although they were considered by their authors to be ethnographic studies of, to use Stanley Fish's phase, 'interpretative communities' (Fish 1980), their approaches differed in important ways. The basic technique used in several of these studies was the analysis of letters, but, it is argued, rigorous ethnography requires the researcher being several months 'in the field' with the respondents in their 'natural' environment.

Hall posited an interpretive interaction between producers and audience, but in his model they do not have the equivalence they had earlier. It posits a series of *professional codes* through which the text is constructed. These are something other than the textual codes that underpin the formal structure of the text. Hall is referring to the codification of institutional production practices that are learned by programme makers, journalists, etc., in the course of their careers. Interpretative acts are also codified. It is with these that Hall introduces an interface between interpretation, and the social and ideological position of the audience.

Hall described three broad classes of reading based on:

- dominant codes;
- negotiated codes;
- oppositional codes.

The *dominant* is where the **preferred meaning** is accepted; this corresponds to the intended encoded meaning. A *negotiated reading* is a **partial acceptance** of the preferred reading, but one that is inflected appositionally. The *oppositional* reading is a reading that **deliberately inverts the preferred reading**.

Reader response criticism emerged in the 1960s. A number of European and American literary theorists shifted the focus of meaning in a literary text away from the author to that of the reader. In their various ways, Barthes, Iser, Fish and others reconfigured the relationship between reader and text. The act of reading was presented as a *negotiation* between text and reader;

meaning was no longer conceived as lying immanent in a text, waiting to be excavated. Meaning was *what happened* between the reader and text: 'meaning' became an event or process, a verb rather than a noun, and was seen to lie not so much within words, as in the space between them. One of the problems with effects studies is that they generally do not allow for the reader's interpretative activity; at best they allow for 'noise' (e.g. Shannon and Weaver in McQuail and Windahl 1981, p. 12) which is anything that intercedes between sender and receiver and 'distorts' the message. Uses and gratification, whilst shifting attention away from medium to audience, largely inflected 'uses' in terms of fulfilling 'needs', which is rather a narrow of way of understanding, to use Wolfgang Iser's phrase, 'the act of reading' (Iser 1978). Hall does not deny that a message may have an effect, but he moves away from a behaviourist–stimulus response model to an interpretative framework:

> *the formal rules of discourse and language have to operate. Before this message can have an 'effect' (how ever defined)… It must first be perceived as a meaningful discourse and meaningfully decoded. It is this set of decoded meanings which 'have an effect', influence, entertain, instruct, or persuade with very complex perceptual, cognitive, emotional ideological or behavioural consequences*
> **(Hall 1974, p. 3)**

The *Nationwide* Study

David Morley and Charlotte Brunsdon applied Hall's model in a study of audience responses to *Nationwide* in 1978 with the aim of '…. explaining the programme through what people said about it rather than explaining people through the way they respond to the programme' (p. 59). Previous audience research had either over-emphasised the text (effects theory) or the audience (uses and gratification). Morley aimed to shift the emphasis to an understanding of how the programme and its meanings were experienced by people from different socio-economic groups. *Nationwide* was a BBC early evening news and magazine programme. For the purposes of Morley's research, it was understood as a multiple text, the sum of all its episodes, represented by the one that was selected for use in the project. Morley's research differed from later ethnographical work in that the small groups worked with were not in their normal domestic environments, they were gathered together explicitly for the research Morley had in mind. He decided to work with groups because 'much individually-based interview research is flawed by a focus on individuals as social atoms divorced from their social context' (Morley 1980, p. 33). However, this is just what Morley himself was doing, removing his subjects from their normal social context. This is no less the case because he placed people in groups of a similar social background.

Morley worked with 29 groups, of which 26 featured in his published researched. Each group was defined by a cluster of shared characteristics such as age, ethnicity, occupation, gender, social class and political allegiance. The groups included 'mainly white, male apprentice engineers; non-unionised, with a skilled working class background, aged 20–26. Studying part-time in a midlands polytechnic; predominantly "don't know" or Conservative in political orientation' (Morley, p. 40). Other groups were made up of university students, bank workers, shop stewards, black further education students and others.

Morley's work pointed the way to later ethnographical work which was able to incorporate some of the lessons learned from the *Nationwide* project. Central to Morley's project was ideology. He started from the position that the audience is 'structured discursively prior to encountering the television text' (Nightingale 1996, p. 67). The way the audience is structured accounts for varying interpretations 'and for discrepancies between production intentions and audience readings' (ibid. p. 67), in other words, the distance between the encoded preferred meaning and the way it was interpreted, or 'read', by some audiences. One problem with the

Nationwide project is that Morley does not explain *how* class, ethnicity and other demographic factors affect interpretation. The justification in defining the groups in terms of homogeneous demographic characteristics, such as class, is doubtful.

Ethnological (Ethnographic) Research

Audiences in Revolt

Crossroads: The Drama of a Soap Opera (1982) came out of an unusual research situation. A furore had broken out in the popular press over the sacking of Noele Gordon, who played a central and popular character called Meg Mortimer. Dorothy Hobson saw this as a crisis in relations between the audience and the ATV management. This was a situation in which 'the audience would have to re-shape its Gestalt of the programme, and redefine the nature of the hierarchy of relationships which existed within the dramatic world of the soap opera' (p. 69).

The research was confined to women with whom she viewed and discussed the programme. Her findings were arranged into three categories:

- relations between the audience and the text;

- reasons for watching the programme;

- the women's performance as members of the audience.

For the purpose of the research Hobson did not say how many women were involved in the research or say how long it took, other than it lasted over a long period of time. Her involvement with the woman was different to that of Morley and his research group. There appears to have been a closer involvement between them and

Hobson, as the nature of Hobson's research aims suggested the need for a more intimate ethnological approach. Hobson's interviews combined their thoughts about the programme with information about their personal lives.

Hobson found that their attention was engaged by the 'realism' of the text, a realism judged in terms of social and psychological discourse; their pleasure in this was uninhibited by the programme's technical deficiencies of which they were fully aware. Hobson found that they were 'savvy' viewers rather than the 'mindless' ones of urban mythology. Hobson effectively became a spokesperson for the audience, arguing that they have a different relationship with the programme, built up over a long period of time, than either executives or programme-makers. Holland also considered the role of the programme within the context of the women's domestic lives, noting that family structures and the routine of the home affected the nature of their viewing. Most of the women seemed unable to give exclusive attention to the programme when it was transmitted: it had to be worked into a pattern of domestic activities. It was in the sphere of the domestic that *Crossroads* accrued its meaning for the women. Much of the meaning was extra-textual, the programme being incorporated into domestic conversation. It was the domestic role played by the programme in the lives of the women she interviewed that highlighted their lack of the power. For the elderly and infirm, the programme offered companionship; it was this that was disrupted by the sacking of Gordon.

The Reception of *Dallas*

Another ethnographic study of audiences and popular culture was Ien Ang's *In Watching Dallas: Soap Opera and the Melodramatic Imagination* (1985). The purpose behind the work was to offer a framework within which *Dallas* could be taken seriously (ibid. p. vii). The focus of the analysis was how the programme produced pleasure and was read by its audience. Like *Crossroads,* there was a dismissive climate of opinion around the programme and one of the things that Ang considered was the way in which members of its audience were often secretive about the pleasures they derived from *Dallas*: in a sense her work brought these pleasures 'out of the closet'. The respondents were a small group of self-selected regular *Dallas* viewers. They had replied to an advertisement Ang had placed in a Dutch women's magazine, *Viva*, asking *Dallas* fans to write to her, saying why they liked the programme. The study drew together two distinct threads in media studies: the political economy of the media and feminist criticism.

Some of the problems with the study included:

• sampling: the way letters from viewers were used for information;

• a preference for explanations that emphasised emotion rather than cognition or knowledge;

• minimal use of contemporary psychoanalytic theories.

By the late 1980s the ethnographical approach to audience research was under attack (Ang 1991; Fiske 1988 and Radway 1988). An argument began to emerge that there is no such a thing as a television audience other than being 'a discursive construct' produced by analysis: 'audience' was not so much a material entity as an abstraction. Grossberg, for instance, wrote, 'media audiences are shifting constellations, located within varying multiple discourses which are never entirely outside of the media discourse themselves' (1988, p. 386). Ang's book *Desperately Seeking the Audience* is a sustained exposition of this argument. She offers a deconstruction of the television industry's illusionary pursuit of the 'audience' defined as 'a collection of spectators, a group of individuals who are gathered together to attend a performance and "receive" a message "sent" by another' (Ang 1991, p. 33). It is easy, writes Ang, to conceive of an audience for a football match in this way, 'it is perfectly clear here who the audience is: those who are inside the stadium are, those outside it are not part of it' (ibid., p. 34). With the emergence of a reading public in the eighteenth century, an audience emerged that is 'a much more elusive phenomenon' (ibid.): the mass media audience. The television audience, like any mass media audience (except the cinema audience) 'is characterised by geographical dispersedness [sic]: television spectatorship takes place in a millions of private homes' (ibid.). It also lacks a clearly framed unit of performance; it is instead 'characterised by a constant flow of programmes, segments and items' (ibid.). Television is always there, always accessible; concomitantly, the audience is always present, but it is always changing. It can never be 'pinned' down in either time or location in the way a traditional pre-mass culture audience could.

The third generation of audience studies was not restricted to investigating the reception or 'reading' of a programme by a particular audience, the 'objective is to get a grasp of our contemporary media culture' (Lull 1990, p. 6), to explore the role of the media in everyday life. The interest in programmes and programming was studying texts in the context of their usage as a part of everyday life: 'the central object of analysis of mass communication research lies outside the media, in the cultures and communities of which media and audiences are constituents' (ibid., p. 14). The approach added 'a neglected layer of reflexivity to the reception of media messages by addressing the audience's notions of themselves as the audience' (ibid.).

Theories of Television Violence

Content Analysis

Content analysis is the process of quantifying the recurrence of specified elements in a text. It is a technique that is useful in the study of representation. For example, an analysis of the representation of old age in a soap opera might begin with counting the number of times an old person appears in an episode, or a sequence of episodes: this would indicate the level or degree of representation. The analysis might then proceed to considering the nature of the characters' roles – the kind of activity they engage in, their appearance, etc. Content analysis is a technique often alluded to by critics of screen violence: in essence equivalence is presumed between the number of violent acts present in a text and its potential to cause psychological harm.

The Internet is awash with 'scholarly' articles bemoaning the amount of violence on television (almost exclusively American) and the alleged consequence – an excess of aggression or unruliness in children. There are examples aplenty; one only has to enter 'television violence' in a search engine and there they are in their hundreds. Typical is:

> *According to one estimate, by the time most children leave elementary school they will have seen approximately 8,000 murders and more than 100,000 other acts of violence on television. Such staggering numbers have contributed to a growing public perception that violence on TV has become more pervasive, more graphic and more problematic.*
> **(http://www.childrennow.org/media/medianow/ mnwinter1998.html)**

One of the problems with the casual invocation of this kind of data is that it does not differentiate between different kinds of screen violence, or the context in which it occurs – violence is assumed to be homogeneous. A slap around the face is not the same as a decapitation, and then again, a decapitation in a naturalistic thriller is not the same as a decapitation shown in Bart and Lisa Simpson's favourite cartoon, *Itchy and Scratchy*. In some instances, a slap in the face will be the more disturbing. It is likely that children find depictions of domestic violence, played out in a recognisable environment, more troubling than the goriest acts of death and mayhem, which they realise, are fantasy.

One useful content analysis of British television was undertaken by Guy Cumberbatch in 1987. Cumberbatch occupies an unusual position in the debate on screen violence. He is an applied psychologist, but has been a long-time critic of both the way laboratory experiments have been undertaken, and the way in which their results have been used. Cumberbatch takes the view that there is no conclusive evidence that screen violence is harmful; yet he himself employs laboratory research techniques.

Cumberbatch's own content analysis of British television was not concerned with effects, but to 'remedy some very clear deficiencies in our knowledge: just how much 'violence' is there on television and of what nature is it' (p.1). What Cumberbatch does do, and a great many writers who use content data do not, is place violence in the context of the programme in which it is featured. His study surveyed programme content broadcast on four UK terrestrial channels between 25–31 May; 7–13 July, 2–8 August and 17–23 September 1986. The definition of violence used by Cumberbatch is 'any action of physical force with or without a weapon against oneself or another person, animal or inanimate object, whether carried through or merely attempted and whether the action caused injury or not. Both intentional and accidental violence were included. Violent accidents and catastrophes were also covered but acts of nature were only included as violence if victims were shown. Verbal abuse and threats were coded separately.' (Cumberbatch 1987, p.2) In his analysis, Cumberbatch makes a distinction between violent actions (punching, stabbing, etc), and violent acts 'which refers to a coherent uninterrupted sequence of actions involving the same agents in the same roles' (ibid, p.2). In all, across 2,078 programmes transmitted over 1412 hours there were a 2,375 violent acts. It is this kind of data that proselytisers of anti-screen violence bandy about as if it was in itself conclusive evidence of the potential for 'harm'. But as Cumberbatch writes of his study, 'This research was not designed to produce simplistic summaries of violence regardless of context and style'. Such summaries can be misleading. Cumberbatch attempts to place 'violence counting' within two contexts. First he takes into account the role of violent acts within the drama itself. Beginning with genre and audiences' expectations induced by their knowledge of generic conventions, he goes on to analyse the role of violence within particular dramatic narratives, working to a series of categories based on character types.

Cumberbatch's study is useful in clarifying the amount and kind of violence on television. His is a study that, through a careful collating and analysis of the evidence, seems to show that even on their own terms, the anti-screen violence lobby has over-stated its case.

Four Major Theories of Television Violence
(see: http://www.magicdragon.com/EmeraldCity/Nonfiction/socphil.html)

Arousal
The arousal thesis maintains that exposure to screen violence will increase aggression in the individual by raising levels of excitation, that is to say 'arouses' the viewer. According to this theory, it is not only images of violence that induce aggression, but also the excitation

induced by certain formal properties of film and television, rapid editing, dynamic camera movements and so on.

Social Learning

The central tenet of social learning is that behaviour is learned through observation. Bandura has been a leading exponent of the theory that social observation is one of the means by which children acquire unfamiliar behaviour. This includes observing representations of behaviour on television.

Bandura and the Bobo Doll

Bandura's work on television violence and aggression resulted from his study of whether the attractiveness of a teacher influenced learning. Bandura observed that if the teacher committed any kind of aggressive act it would be imitated. Bandura went on to investigate imitative aggression in which the Bobo (or Bozo) doll played a significant part. In one experiment children were invited to witness an aggravated assault upon a large inflated doll: '.... After addressing the figure belligerently, the model pommels it on the head with a mallet, hurls it down, sits on it and punches it on the nose repeatedly, kicks it across the room, flings it in the air, and bombards it with balls' (Bandura 1973, p. 72 cited in Cumberbatch and Howitt 1989, p. 33). Following on from this spectacle, the children are induced into a state of frustration by being shown some attractive toys, but denied any opportunity to play with them. The children are then shown to another room containing a Bobo doll and other objects of the sort with which the model attacked the doll. Perhaps not surprisingly, the children (88%)'imitated the models and were able to reproduce more than 70% of the responses observed immediately after exposure and even 8 months later may still retain 40% of them' (ibid. p. 33). Children do learn by observation and social learning, but 'there is growing dissatisfaction with the ecological validity of the laboratory experiment: children do not typically imitate all that they see or even attempt to do so' (ibid. p. 35).

The problem with laboratory-based research is that the subjects, the children, are placed in artificial situations far removed from their everyday reality: the television is no longer in a familiar room with the floor, perhaps, littered with familiar toys and the air enriched with the sounds and smells of home. Instead, the young child is confronted with something far more alien.

In another experiment Bandura showed some children a violent cartoon film: others were shown a non-violent film. All of them were placed in a room with large soft dolls. Bandura noted that those children who had seen the violent film were the more aggressive and he concluded from this that the violent cartoons had caused the children to behave more aggressively.

There are several issues concerning these experiments (as with all laboratory experiments). They do not differentiate between short- and long-term effects. 'Violence' seems to be regarded homogeneously by Bandura. Can a child 'aggressively' playing with a toy be compared with real-life violence? Is it reasonable to assume that the play will carry over to real-life situations?

The problem with Bandura's work, and other laboratory-based research is precisely that: the context of 'the observed stimuli' (Comstock and Lindsey, 1975, p. 27) is the artificial environment of the laboratory, removed from any real social situation. As Fowles puts it, 'laboratory experiments on violence are concocted schemes that violate all the essential stipulations of actual viewing in the real world' (Fowles, 1999, p. 27). Aside from the artificiality of laboratory experiments, there are two other problems. The first is 'experimenter expectancy bias' (Rosnow and Rosenthal 1997, p. 3 cited in Fowles 1999, p. 27). This is where the expectations, or 'premonitions' (ibid. p. 27), of experimenters are realised in their results. Fowles argues that 'There is good reason to believe that experimenter expectancy bias may have tainted the results of many laboratory studies on media-inspired aggression because many academic researchers harbour suspicions about the excesses of popular entertainment' (ibid. p. 27).

Second is the 'good subject effect': subjects' behaviour will conform to what they perceive is demanded of them by the experimenter – the 'demand characteristics of the experimental situation' (Rosnow and Rosenthal, 1997 cited in Fowles 1999, p. 28). Fowles illustrates this by referring to work carried out by Richard Borden. Borden found that in an experiment designed to calibrate levels of aggression, the behaviour of the subjects was influenced by the gender of the experimental observer. 'In sum, the results indicated that the subjects' aggressive behaviour was apparently a function of their expectations of approval for such behaviour based on the inferred or explicit values of the observer' (ibid. p. 28). Fowles, drawing on numerous experiments, shows that so 'wayward is the laboratory experimental situation that many anomalous findings regarding aggression have been derived' (ibid. p. 28)

Disinhibition

Another frequently cited name associated with laboratory-based research and learning theory is Leonard Berkowitz. Berkowitz's field of interest lay not so much in the role of screen violence in inducing aggressive impulses, but in that of reducing them. He was unconvinced by the thesis that 'fantasy behaviour performed a drive-reducing (cathartic) function', that is say that watching a violent film reduced aggression. Berkowitz thought that any such reduction in aggression was more likely 'due to the film heightening a subject's anxiety about his own display of aggression rather than the aggression becoming vicariously discharged due to the film' (Cumberbatch 1989, p. 34).

The disinhibition hypothesis posits that television violence can result in increased interpersonal aggression, because it weakens an individual's inhibitions against such behaviour (Berkowitz 1962).

The findings so far suggest that such circumstances include those in which the television violence is rewarded, those in which cues similar to

those in television portrayal appear in the environment, and those in which the environment contains a target who has previously provoked or harmed the viewer. Like Tannenbaum and Bandura, Berkowitz believes in testing hypotheses in order to construct theory and in rigorous control in order to infer cause and effect. However, unlike Tannenbaum, he has been interested in the direct contribution of television violence to the performance of acquired behaviour. And unlike both Tannenbaum and Bandura, his most recent research has involved naturalistic field experiments on the effects of television violence of subsequent interpersonal aggression.
(Comstock and Lindsey 1975, p. 27)

It would seem unwise to make a general extrapolation from Berkowita's research that television violence itself *causes* aggression. Berkowitz seems to be making the unsurprising claim, that in quite particular circumstances, images of television violence can be found amongst a constellation of factors that lead to aggressive behaviour.

Desensitisation

Associated with disinhibition is the claim that prolonged and extensive exposure to media violence reduces sensitivity to *real* violence. As with disinhibition, or, for that matter, any other attested media effect, evidence for this is questionable. A problem for any researcher in proving such a hypothesis is the nature of any longitudinal research. Any behaviour trait will be determined by an intractable host of 'causes' – personal history, psychology and so forth. How does one remove from the 'experiment' all of the other variables, leaving only media effects? It can't be done. There is also the 'chicken and egg' problem: do people behave violently, because they watch a lot of TV violence or do they watch a lot of TV violence because they themselves are violent?

Belson's Experiment

In 1978 Belson published the findings of his study of 1,565 London boys aged between 12 and 17. This was an attempt to correlate violent behaviour with TV viewing and also to determine whether exposure to TV violence would lead to a desensitisation to real violence. He checked the boys' recall of 100 programmes that were screened on television between 1959 and 1971. The programmes were graded for violent content on a ten-point scale. On the one hand, he found no correlation between 'levels of television violence viewing and callousness to real violence or inconsiderateness to others' (Fowles 1999, p. 29) but he did find that those with the highest levels of exposure to TV violence committed 49% more acts of serious violence than those who watched less. Fowles, however, persuasively demonstrates that Belson's conclusion is not valid. According to Fowles (1999), Belson's data, surprisingly, suggests that *low* viewers of television violence are more aggressive than moderate viewers. Furthermore, moderate viewers seemed to have shown more aggression than *high* volume viewers. This reading of Belson's data seems to contradict his actual finding. Fowles highlights what seems to be a highly selective way in which he employed three categories. 'Serious violence', which was singled out in his findings, was one of four categories, the others being:

- 'total number of acts of violence';

- 'total number of acts of violence weighted by degree of severity of the act;

- 'total number of violent acts excluding minor ones.

The findings for these three do not support Belson's conclusion. In fact Fowles shows that there is a *reverse* correlation. 'Three of his measures refuted his argument, but Belson chose to emphasize the fourth, itself a demonstrably inconsistent measure' (1999, p. 31).

Aggression Reduction/'Catharsis'

The cathartic principle of drama goes back to Aristotle, who argued that when an audience becomes emotionally involved with a story, climaxes of aggression or excitement lead to a 'catharsis' or release of emotion which is not only pleasurable, but reduces levels of emotional energy. Sometimes referred to as the aggression reduction hypothesis, it has been posited as an alternative way of understanding the effect of screen violence. Feshbach (Fowles 1999, p. 30) argues that television violence diminishes violent impulses by supplying material for aggressive fantasies, which thereby diminish aggressive impulses in the individual. Another condition is said to occur when television violence creates aggression anxiety, leading to the inhibition of aggressive impulses within the individual. There are echoes of this in Freud, who argued that unless 'people were allowed to express themselves aggressively, the aggressive energy would be dammed up, pressure would build, and the aggressive energy would seek an outlet, either exploding into acts of extreme violence or manifesting itself as symptoms of mental illness' (Aronson 1995, p. 258). Aronson goes on to argue, reasonably enough, that there is no conclusive evidence for this hypothesis. It's interesting, however, that the lack of conclusive evidence does not inhibit exponents of the hypothesis from asserting that television actually causes aggression (Comstock and Lindsey, 1975).

One of the ironies of the many outpourings on effects studies, especially those tied to studies of television and violence, is that many of the authorities their authors cite were themselves very cautious in their conclusions. One of the most exhaustive studies undertaken on the effects of television violence was that submitted to the US Surgeon General's Scientific Advisory Committee on Television and Social Behaviour in 1972. The 12-member panel included Thomas Coffin, a psychologist who was Vice President for Research at NBC, and Joseph Klapper, a sociologist who was Director of the Office of Social Research at CBS. Submitted after three years of research and including over 60 reports, it contained a massive amount of evidence and yet offered a no more conclusive finding than television *might*, in some instances, influence children negatively. The results of the report provided no more certainty than there was before it was undertaken, yet it has often been cited as providing conclusive evidence of the causal relationship between screen violence and aggression. The summary of the report included:

We have noted in the studies at hand a modest association between viewing of violence and aggression among at least some children, and we have noted some data which are consonant with the interpretation that viewing violent programs produces the aggression; this evidence is not conclusive, however, and some of the data are also consonant with other interpretations.
(cited in Fowles 1999, p. 8)

It seems that the senator who instigated the report, John Pastore of Rhode Island, was not at all happy with this conclusion. Fowles shows that he not only reconvened the hearings, but by orchestrating 'witnesses and the news media's response to them, Pastore was able to recast the report as a clear indictment of television violence' (1999, p. 10). At the reconvened hearing and under 'direct questioning', Pastore managed to elicit from the Surgeon General, Jesse Steinfeld, a more emphatic statement: 'Certainly my interpretation is that there is a causative relationship between televised violence and subsequent antisocial behaviour, and the evidence is strong that it requires some action on the part of responsible authorities, the TV industry, the government, and citizens' (cited by Fowles 1999, p. 10).

The V-Chip: Controlling the Viewing of Violence

One of the eventual outcomes of concerns raised by TV violence has been the controversy over the V-Chip in the USA. The Telecommunications Act of 1996 was signed by President Clinton in February of that year. It was a wide ranging act, that at one and the same time offered the telecommunications industry a measure of deregulation and a response to the increasing pubic concern over television violence – the V-Chip. The V-Chip, developed by Professor Tim Collings of Simon Fraser University in Canada, allows a parent to set the television to block out unwanted programming. The V-Chip is technology built into a TV set that 'reads' the rating for a particular TV programme. Television manufacturers have been required to place a V-Chip in all television sets larger than 13 inches since the middle of 1998.

The V-Chip can be set to block programmes with any given rating, including talk shows, soap operas, sitcoms, dramas and films. Sport and news programmes are not rated. Children's programmes are divided into two age categories: TV-Y and TV-Y7. A TV-Y rating means that the programme is considered to be appropriate for children of all ages. The TV-Y7 rating is for children aged seven and older. Controversially, children younger than seven are regarded as being unable to differentiate between fiction and reality. TV Parental Guidelines have one or more letters added to the basic rating to indicate when a programme contains higher levels of violence, sex, swearing or suggestive dialogue:

Therefore a TV-Y7-FV rating indicates that a programme may contain some or all of the following: violence is a prevalent feature of the programme; fighting is presented in an exciting way; villains and heroes are valued for their fighting abilities; violent acts are glorified; violence is depicted as an acceptable and effective solution to a problem.

The TV Parental Guidelines are voluntary and not all broadcasters use them. In order to block any unedited film shown on cable channels, the V-Chip can be set for the Motion Picture Association of America (MPAA) film ratings. Welcomed by some, the government and FCC has been accused of ducking the question of violence on television and caving into the telecommunications industry by shifting the responsibility to parents. While this might very well be seen as being where the responsibility belongs, concerns have been raised:

The V-Chip will 'put the remote control back in the hands of parents,' says President Clinton. Yet its moral compass points in the opposite direction: instead of empowering parents or strengthening their influence in America's cultural landscape, the V-Chip challenges parental authority and places them in an untenable position: holding their own against the relentless wave of commercial exploitation from outside, while fighting an adversarial war to suppress their child's innate desire to experience the forbidden world.
(Brian Burke, Director of Centre for Educational Priorities, http://www.vchipeducation.org)

Fowles argues that the V-Chip 'is another weapon in the generation war' that can only increase hostility between parents and children: 'not only will normal levels of tension and animosity be denied their outlet via television fiction, but also so will the new superheated levels. It is not a congenial prospect' (Fowles 1999, p. 129).

Since 2003 the V-Chip has been supplemented by the Television Guardian, outlined below in a web advertisement (http://www.familysafemedia.com):

How does the TVGuardian work?
TVGuardian uses the hidden closed caption signal to find profanity. The process consists of monitoring the closed captioned signal, each captioned word is checked against a dictionary of offensive words stored in the TVGuardian. If an offensive word is detected, the audio is muted for the sentence, the offensive word is removed from the closed captioned signal. A suitable word is substituted for the profanity, when appropriate, and the replacement sentence is displayed on the screen in text form.

Example:
In the movie Mrs. Doubtfire, *'You bring home the "gd" zoo', would be silenced. The words, 'You*

bring home the zoo', would be displayed in closed-caption on the TV.

Rhett Butler has never given a d***. That's why Family Safe Media sells a black box called TVGuardian that mutes out a program's offensive language and changes it for a filtered closed-caption version.

In August 1997, captioning was made mandatory for most television programmes including old ones such as *I Love Lucy*. TVGuardian cannot work with live broadcasts (sport and news) as they do not use closed captioning. A DVD player with a similar censoring function is ClearPlay, which is 'pre-programmed to edit about 500 titles. By inserting ordinary DVDs of these films, consumers will be able to select from 14 levels of filtering. Choose the top level and you might wonder what will be left of some of Hollywood's more lurid offerings' (*The Guardian*, 11 April 2004). At the time of writing, 'several leading Hollywood figures... including Steven Spielberg and Steven Soderberg, are backing a lawsuit, arguing that the technology will violate the rights of directors who expect their works to be viewed in their entirety, without censorship' (ibid, 2004).

Audience Measurement

Ratings

Ratings are generally regarded as being synonymous with audience research. They are not, of course, insofar as ratings measurement is only one feature of audience research, if the most high profile one. Even within the organisations that produce ratings, such as Nielsen and Arbitron, they are only one of many research products derived from the huge amount of data that is collected. Within the broadcasting industries, especially in America, they have a singular potency: 'Ratings are a powerful force in broadcasting and communications. They determine the price that will be paid for programs and the pay that performers will receive. They govern the rates that advertisers will pay for 60-second or 30-second or smaller commercial units in and around each program. Ratings determine stations' audience and rank order in their market, and to a large degree they dictate the profitability of broadcasting stations and their value when they are put up for sale' (Barwise and Ehrenberg 1988, p. 10).

Ratings originated in the USA in the 1930s in response to the growth in radio as a mass advertising medium. The problem with radio was that, unlike the theatre, cinema and the press, there was no evident way of gaining a reliable estimate of how many people were listening. Broadcasters have a number of audience research needs:

• the appeal of new programmes have to be tested;

- long-running programmes have to be re-tested (*maintenance* research). This includes measuring the appeal of storylines and characters. It is also used by politicians to measure the response to speeches, party political broadcasts, etc.;

- studying audience flow from one channel or programme to another. For the larger US networks and advertisers this can be very sophisticated research, involving large amounts of data and mathematical models;

- understanding more about how people use and respond to television.

However, as a commercial enterprise, the principal aim of (non-Public Service) broadcasters is to sell audiences to advertisers. By the same token, they must first acquire an audience, and one as large as possible. The larger an audience that can be sold to advertisers, the higher the rate they can be charged. As American broadcasting is the most outright commercial, as well as being the largest, they developed the most sophisticated marketing and research system. In the USA there are three distinct broadcasting markets:

- the national market place;

- local markets;

- national spot and regional markets.

The National Market
This is the largest and most lucrative, controlled by four national networks: ABC, CBS, NBC and Fox Television. The national market is subdivided into smaller markets called *dayparts*. A daypart is a portion of the broadcast schedule defined by time and programme content. Each daypart is defined by its own set of characteristics and appeals to different advertisers. They generate different amounts of money and will have different rates of charges to advertisers.

The dayparts are:

- prime time – between 8 p.m. and 11 p.m. Mon–Sat; 7 p.m.–11 p.m. Sunday;

- daytime – between 7 a.m. and 4:30 p.m. Mon–Fri;

- sports;

- news;

- late night – 11:30 p.m. until early morning Mon–Fri;

- children.

Prime time
This is the most important of the network dayparts. Prime time is attractive to those advertisers who wish to appeal to the widest variety of people, nationwide. This is also the only time when advertisers can reach people who have the highest disposable income, mostly those who are working during the day.

Daytime
The smaller audience means that 'spots' are cheaper and appeals to those advertisers who wish to reach women who do not work away from home.

Sports
Prime time and daytime markets are defined by time; sports is defined by content. The most expensive spots fall between the major league games, the National Football League, the National Basketball Association and with baseball, the World Series. The fees for key games can be huge: the fee for a 30 second spot during the Super Bowl can exceed a million dollars. The audience is predominately male and 'spots' are largely bought by brewers, car manufactures, etc.

News
Like sports, this daypart is defined by content. It includes
the national networks evening news programmes,
weekend news, news specials and documentaries. Not
included in this daypart are the morning news
programmes (these are counted as day time) and major
current affairs programmes such as *60 Minutes*, which
are included in prime time.

Late night
Late night has a small adult audience for programmes
such as the *Late Show with David Letterman* and *The
Tonight Show with Jay Leno*. Small though the audience
generally is, it is still an attractive one for many
advertisers, as the demographics suggest high earners.

Children
Mostly scheduled Saturday and Sunday mornings, this
daypart can also include weekday programmes aimed at
children. This daypart tends to be subjected to close
scrutiny by public interest groups and government
regulators. Demand tends to be seasonal, with Christmas
attracting the highest rates.

Buying airtime
Markets are also defined by when advertisers buy
airtime. There are three such markets:

- upfront;
- scatter;
- opportunistic.

Upfront
This is the first round of buying, which occurs in the
spring and summer. The more time that is sold at this
stage the better it is for the broadcasters, as it is not
known how well programmes will do, especially new
ones (advertisers are less likely to buy time once a series
has started to run if it is not doing well). In return for

agreeing to buy time over the coming year, advertisers acquire spots in the most attractive programmes at discounted rates. Sometimes, to make the deal even more attractive, advertisers will be offered a guaranteed minimum audience. If this is not achieved within the amount of time purchased, the advertisements continue to run for free: these are called *make-goods.*

Scatter

Scatter markets are closer to the transmission time of the programmes. Each television season is divided into quarters. Advertisers can buy time in advance of each one. Scatter markets are useful for those advertisers, especially of seasonal products, who do not require year long advertising. Scatter markets are also used to buy extra time. Generally, in terms of the price of advertising time, scatter markets work to the advantage of the seller, especially if it is a strong season and programmes are doing well. On the other hand, if they are not doing so well, the advantage can shift to the buyer.

Opportunistic

These markets occur within the television season. They can work to the mutual advantage of buyers and sellers. Advertisers who need time are able to fill a void where spots have either not been sold or deals have fallen through.

Syndication

The starting point for the structure of any broadcasting system is how to utilise the spectrum of wavelength that is assigned to each nation internationally. In the 1920s, the decision in the UK was to create a monopoly – the BBC. In the US, they went the other way and created a wholly commercial system administered by a government agency, the Federal Communications Commission (FCC). The organising principal was, and remains, to license radio and television stations in specific cities and towns. Larger urban areas have more stations. The major rating services such as Nielsen use these regions as boundaries for their own designated market areas (DMAs). Charges for advertising spots are partly determined by the size and demographics of each DMA. In New York, for example, there are in excess of seven million households with televisions; in North Platte there are fewer than 20,000. Advertising on a New York station will reach more people than some national cable networks whereas a market as small as North Platte will be too small to be economically measured. There are huge national differences; a 30 second spot in Des Moines might only be $400, but in Detroit it could cost $4,000. But there are other factors that determine the cost of time, such as whether the market is expanding or shrinking and the competitiveness of local media – even the time zone can make a difference.

The national structure of American television is based on syndication. Independently owned television and radio stations affiliate themselves to one of the national networks in order to acquire their programming. This is a mutually advantageous arrangement as it guarantees the station programming, while at the same time creating national markets for the networks. National markets are largely a constellation of local markets. There is a similar structure in cable: 'Broadcast networks reach national markets by combining the audiences of the local stations with which they affiliate. Similarly, national cable networks aggregate the viewers of local cable systems' (Webster et al. 2000, p. 20).

Internet

Internet use has expanded to the point where the equivalent of a ratings system is being developed for the benefit of advertisers and site owners alike. There are a number of agencies now involved in developing a means of measuring the exposure that websites receive, such as the Internet Advertising Bureau and traditional ratings companies such as Arbitron. Measurement is along the lines of radio and television, including reach, frequency of hits, user share, weighted examples, etc. Websites can be represented by firms that provide a range of services, in particular the soliciting of advertising. Up to a point, website operators have the means of doing their own research by collating data from cookies. Every time a user visits a site, it is logged in the form of a cookie. But as a measurement tool, they are unreliable as they can be blocked and neither is there any way of identifying who used the computer with cookies alone.

Research Questions

Whatever the medium, there are some basic questions that audience research needs to answer.

Audience size

Audience size, represented by the ratings, determines the value of television and radio to advertisers. The baseline for the rating figure is the TV/radio owning population. The rating is a projected percentage of this population that is tuned into a particular station, extrapolated from a demographically selected sample. One rating point is one per cent of the TV/radio owning households. 'Rating' can, however, mean something different entirely – it can be an expression of the actual audience share, that is to say a percentage of the population *using* television at that time, rather than *owning* one – this is a percentage of the *actual* rather than *potential* audience.

'Population' can also be interpreted differently. It can either refer to the number of television owning households or be an absolute figure representing the number of individuals in the audience. Either way, they are both numbers derived from the same data, expressing the size of the audience. Any one rating figure will have different values depending on the size of the market: a rating of 15 in New York will represent a higher absolute number of audience members than a rating of 25 in North Platte. The number of households using television or radio at any given moment is the *households using television (or radio)* (HUT/HUR) level. This can also be expressed as an absolute number: *persons using television (or radio)* (PUR/PUR). These levels vary throughout the day, in predictable ways, from hour to hour. HUT levels are prefered to ratings, as they give a 'truer' indication of how many people are actually watching (or listening, in the case of radio). As audience share does not indicate the absolute audience size, buyers and sellers of air time use both HUT/PUTs and shares to estimate predicted ratings.

Another figure of which advertisers are very mindful is the *gross rating point* (GRP). What is significant to a campaign is not the number of people who see any single transmission of an advertisement, but the number who are exposed, overall, throughout the whole campaign. This is expressed by the GRP, which is a measure of the total audience. The GRP, however, must be carefully interpreted: a GRP of 100 might mean that 100% of the audience has seen the advertisement, or it might only mean that 1% of the audience has seen it 100 times!

How often do the same people appear in the audience?

It is important that researchers know how much *audience duplication* there is: are programmes with the same rating seen by different or the same groups of people? Advertisers want to how many different people (*reach*) have seen the advertisement and how many (*frequency*).

- *reach* – number of unduplicated individuals who see an advertisement (cumulative rating), with the Internet this is defined as unique visitors;

- *frequency* – how many times did each individual see the ad – this varies across different media (Webster, et al. 2000, p. 30).

Is there a typical audience member?

Advertisers need to know that they are reaching their target audience. Different advertisers want to reach different kinds of audience. Knowledge about the constitution of the audience is as important as its size, sometimes more so. An advertiser may be more interested in reaching a smaller, but high spending audience than a large but low spending one. Broadcasters and advertisers are increasingly able to gather a great deal of information about their audience and markets, made easier by modern communications technology. For advertisers, the 'mass' audience is a misnomer. Advertisers break the audience down into segments, each defined by a number of variables included in ratings books, such as:

- gender;

- age;

- income;

- marital status;

- occupations;

- geographic location;

- behavioural variables (media use).

Audience fragmentation and the ability of modern technology to configure a product to suit the requirements of the individual consumer, have led to a reformulation of the concept of 'mass production'. 'If, as telecommunications companies envision, the Internet is eventually to become the platform for the delivery of all forms of home entertainment, every customized set of viewing preferences will be recorded by service providers' (Andrejevic 2004, p. 43). This will mean the acquisition of a great deal of information about individual consumers, which can be used for the purpose of targeting them with specific, even customised advertisements.

Programming

Audience research is as important for programmers as it is for advertisers. The broadcaster has to attract the largest possible number of the intended audience in order to sell the programme to the advertisers. Audience research needs to answer a number of basic questions for the broadcaster:

- Did I attract the intended audience?

- How loyal is my audience?

- What other stations or programmes does my audience use?

- How will structural factors like scheduling affect programme audience formation?

- When will a programme's costs exceed it benefits? (Webster, et al. 2000, p. 50)

Audience Measurement Techniques

Telephone recall
The method that was developed and refined in the 1930s by Crossley was *telephone recall*. By 1935 such surveys were being conducted for CBS and NBC in 33 cities. The system was to telephone respondents four times a day, asking them to recall the programmes to which they had listened during the previous three to six hours. The problem with telephone recall was that although radio ownership was widespread, this was the not the case with telephones: much of the radio audience was not reachable with this method.

Another problem with Crossley's method was that it depended upon the listener being able to remember exactly what they had listened to. George Gallop had an answer to this, although his method still depended upon the use of the telephone. Gallop measured audience size with what became known as coincidental telephone surveying; this involved simply asking people what they were listening to at the time of the call. He first used this method in 1927, when he was at Drake University and then while working for an advertising agency. There were other pioneers of this method including Pauline Arnold, Percival White and John Karol (who would later become director of research at CBS). Arnold undertook a comparative study of telephone recall and coincidental telephone surveys. She found that the coincidental method had distinct advantages over recall. With the recall method, some programmes were under-reported when compared with the coincidental method, for example, drama was better remembered than music programmes.

In 1933, after a period of running his own research company (specialising in magazines who were concerned that radio was 'getting all of the advertising dollars') Claude Hooper further developed the coincidental method for radio. He devised four questions:

1. Were you listening to the radio just now?

2. To what programme were you listening?

3. Over what station is that programme coming?

4. What the advertiser puts on that programme? (Walker et al. 2000, p. 85)

In addition, respondents were asked the number of men, women and children who were listening. Regarded as being more accurate than CAB, Hooper's system quickly established itself as the industry standard and became widely known as the *Hooperatings*. For the radio industry, Hooper had another advantage: CAB was inextricably tied in with the advertising industry, after all, that was how it started. Hooper, on the other hand, served advertisers and the broadcast industry, providing audience measurement information for both. Hooper was also an accomplished publicist and succeeded in promoting Hooperatings not only within the industry, but also among the pubic. They virtually entered popular culture via the popular press and radio. He introduced the 'pocketpiece' format for ratings data which included information such as 'available audience', 'sets in use' and 'percentage of listeners – now referred to as 'audience share' – and the composition of the audience in terms of age and gender. Broadcasting Audience research had evolved into its present day pattern. After WWII, Hooper bought out CAB. Hooper, in his turn, was taken over by the company, in the USA at least, that has become synonymous with television ratings – Nielsen.

Diaries and listening habits
In the earliest days of radio, before the 1920s when the BBC started and the three national networks in the USA, it was an amateur affair with enthusiasts listening in to as many stations as possible, rather like 'radio hams' do today. They kept logs that included radio call signs and place of origin. It was the radio equivalent of train spotting, but it was the origin of one of the mainstays of audience research that is still, in greatly modified form, used today. Ironically, although the use of diaries began in radio, their use did not become widespread until the emergence of television.

The first systematic use of diaries was in the late 1930s. In 1937 Garent Harrison of the University of Michigan began to 'experiment developing a radio research technique for measurement of listening habits which would be inexpensive and yet fairly reliable' (Garrison, 1939 p. 204 cited in Walker et al. 2000, p. 91). The diary had a number of merits. It was relatively cheap and none were excluded as with systems that depended upon the telephone. It could be sent and retrieved by mail. It could include a list of programmes and so did not depend entirely on the respondents' memory, as with the coincidental method. Harrison asked respondents to list the programmes they had listened to, the station and the number of people who were listening. 'With careful attention to correct sampling, distribution of listening tables, and tabulation of raw data, the technique of "listening tables" should assist materially in obtaining at small cost quite detailed information about radio listening' (ibid., p. 205). CBS experimented with using diaries in order to track audience composition and flow. In the late 1940s Hooper started using diaries in areas of low telephone usage. By the late 1940s diaries became the primary method of research. Other people were beginning to prosper in the expanding area of audience research.

In the 1940s James Seller was backed by NBC to test diaries for television. He was sufficiently persuaded by their merits to set up his own company, American Research Bureau (ARB), which was based in Washington. In 1951 ARB expanded when it merged with another company, Tele-Que, who had been using the diary method since 1947. ARB was now the Nielsen's main competitor in the local TV audience measurement business. Its position was consolidated in the 1955 when it took over Hooper's local TV ratings business. By 1961 it was measuring every TV market at least twice a year.

In 1965 ARB started producing local radio reports, and soon became the main provider. ARB's next major development anticipated the modern meter, one that was able to transmit its information directly down telephone lines. In 1957 it was in use in 300 homes and they were able to provide ratings data the day after a broadcast. Although Nielsen held a patent on just about every metering system in use, this was one he did not have; he was compelled to pay ARB a fee for its rights. Ten years later, in 1967, ARB was merged with a computer company, Control Data Corporation. In 1973 they changed their name to Arbitron and abandoned TV monitoring in order to concentrate on local radio, the field in which they are currently the dominant company.

The Meter

Since the 1930s Arthur C. Nielsen had been developing a method of measuring audiences that held out the promise of overcoming the limitations of both the recall and coincidental methods that both depended upon the telephone. This was a metering device that would automatically record what was being watched on television. Other methods were also being developed, in particular the personal interview.

Nielsen was not working alone on the concept of the meter. In 1920 Claude Robinson (later a partner of George Gallup) patented a device to 'provide for scientifically measuring the broadcast listener response by making a comparative record of … receiving sets… tuned over a selected period of time' (Beville 1988, p. 17. cited in Webster et al. 2000, p. 88). The patent was purchased by RCA but nothing more was heard of it. Frank N. Stanton developed a device that was used to compare listening as recorded on questionnaires. He found that people under-estimated the time they spent listening to the radio. A major deficiency with his device was that it did not record the station to which the radio was tuned. However, the instrument developed by Robert Elder and Louis Woodruff in 1934 could. This was the Audiometer. In 1936 Nielsen acquired the rights to the Audiometer. He redesigned it and in 1942 he launched Nielsen Radio Index (NRI), a survey based on 800 homes equipped with the new device. The information was recorded on paper tape that had to be collected. Nielsen turned this necessity into an opportunity to gather information on purchasing habits by doing an inventory on each households 'pantry'. By the 1950s Nielsen had expanded to the point where he was able to buy out Hooper's national rating service and start Nielsen Television Index (NTI). By now he had also improved the technology. A new version of the Audimeter made its recordings on a 16mm film cartridge that households could return by post, thus speeding up the process of data collection.

By the 1960s he was using a **recordmeter** that monitored hours of television usage and also flashed a light as reminder to viewers to fill in their diary. In 1964 Nielsen withdrew from radio monitoring to concentrate on television. By the early 2000s Arbitron Inc (formerly Radio's All Dimension Audience Research (RADAR) and Nielsen Media Research had developed the Portable People Meter which is intended to measure television, radio and cable television audiences. As of 2003, they were at the stage of trying to improve response rates before putting it to wide-scale use.

The Audience Measurement Business

Both in the UK and the USA, the audience measurement business is dominated by a few companies. The main operator in America is Nielsen Media Research. Formerly part of A.C. Nielsen it is now an independent company, it has expanded and now includes Internet and other new media. Nielsen itself was bought by VNU, a Dutch company, in 1999. Arbitron is owned by Ceridian and not only remains involved in measuring local radio, also in the Internet. SRE measures network radio listening. These firms provide 'the currency for the sale of advertising time in the traditional mass media: ratings' (Webster et al. 2000, p. 95). There are a number of smaller companies that offer research services that complement rather than compete with those provided by the larger companies. For example, Accu Track, rather than concentrating on the demographics and numbers of the audience, studies the 'awareness and behaviour of radio listeners'.

BARB Data

BARB (Broadcasters' Audience Research Board) provides television audience research for television channels within the UK. BARB was set up in 1981 to undertake audience measurement for both television and the advertising industry. It is owned by BBC, ITV, Channel 4, Channel 5, BSkyB and the Institute of Practitioners in Advertising. Prior to 1981, the BBC and independent television had their own separated audience research facilities.

Since 2000, BARB's methodology has undergone some changes. It has increased its sample from the previous 4,300 to over 5,000. BARB has installed 5,250 households with metering equipment, but quality control checks mean that not all of them can yet be included in the viewing figures. The initial sample was 3,800 homes, including 1,600 multi-channel homes. The panel is designed to be representative of each ITV and BBC region.

The panel is selected using a multi-stage sample design, maximising the representation of households across the country. This ensures that the panel is fully representative of households across the whole of the UK. Each panel is maintained against a range of individual and household characteristics. These *panel controls* are derived from both the national Census and BARB's own Establishment Survey. This is an ongoing survey, involving around 50,000 interviews a year and is able to identify any changes within the characteristics of the population. The Establishment Survey is also used to recruit households for the survey panel.

Data is collected using a 'peoplemeter' monitoring system. All of the television receiving equipment in each household, including video cassette recorders, set-top box decoders, etc., are monitored. The 'peoplemeter' automatically records the channel to which each television is tuned. It also monitors VCR activity (recording, playback, etc.) including 'time shifting'; it is able to 'fingerprint' videotapes and identify them when played back. Whenever a television is on, all those present, including guests, register their presence by pressing the appropriate button on a handset. Throughout the day, the meter records all viewing that takes place within the household. During the night, the data is transmitted down the telephone to a processing centre to produce 'overnight' viewing data.

Measuring Television Audiences: How Many are Watching?

For most of its relatively brief history audience measurement has been concerned with one specific aspect of the audience: size. Broadcasters go to great lengths – and expense – in order to determine, as accurately as possible, the number of people watching and listening. The impetus behind this was originally commercial, although in the 1930s public service broadcasters also became involved in audience measurement. The motivation for PBS broadcasters engaging in audience research is different to that of commercial television. The need for commercial broadcasters has always been to provide the evidence that they are able to deliver to advertisers and sponsors the largest possible audience: the larger the audience, the higher the rates for advertising spots charged by broadcasters.

In the early 1920s, there was some debate about the function of radio in America. There were those that thought that it should have a public service function and be utilised in the service of education, it quickly evolved as a highly competitive commercial system. From the beginning it was financed through sponsorship and advertising, as was television when the licence was awarded by the FCC in 1940. American television is the only one in the world to have begun as a wholly commercial system; what there is of public service broadcasting started some time afterwards.

The commercial basis of US broadcasting created an almost immediate requirement for audience research. Sponsorship and advertising created a need for a means of reliably estimating the size of audience. The whole point of radio as an advertising medium was its potential for huge exposure: a few seconds of an advertisement or the sound of the company's or product's name that was attached to a sponsored programme would by heard by millions – so it was hoped. The sponsors/advertisers wanted the evidence as did the broadcasters, as the greater the audience, the more that could be charged.

The earliest means of eliciting information about the audience were understandably crude, as in the early 1920s when radio broadcasting began in the USA and UK, no methodology more sophisticated than asking people to write in had been worked out. By the 1920s, AT & T began charging clients a fee for making announcements on their behalf (putative radio adds) this proved to be an effective revenue earner. Towards the end of the 1920s, radio had established itself as a medium both in the UK and the USA. There was still some debate over whether or not radio should be used for education and other public service functions, but the depression put paid to that: broadcasters wanted the financial benefits from advertising. Programme formats were developed with advertising in mind and sponsorship sought. There were, however, no reliable measures of audience size, there was no equivalent to the Audit Bureau of Circulation who were able to provide data on theatre and cinema audience size; they were even able to measure playing of records through sales and jukebox plays – not a reliable measure of the maximum number of plays, but it did provide a kind of minimum baseline.

As we have seen, the BBC was not interested. This meant that the US was the first in the field; they had, after all, the strongest motivation. To begin with it was little more than counting fan mail and the number of receivers sold, and offering prizes to encourage people to write in with their opinions of programmes. In 1933 the majority of NBC advertisers were engaged in these modest inducements, giving away mostly novelty items of one kind or another. 'Sometimes these were overwhelming. In response to one announcement on a children's programme, WLW in Cincinnati received more than 20,000 letters. The sponsor, Hires Root Beer, used these to select specific stations on which to advertise' (Webster et al. 2000, p. 83). However, there were risks. Ovaltine, who sponsored a production of the children's classic *Little Orphan Annie*, rashly requested that fans 'send in labels in order to free Annie from kidnappers'. This led to an explosion of protest from outraged parents.

While these methods may have indicated what some people thought of the programmes, it did not give anything like an accurate estimate of how many people were actually listening. The larger networks began to develop more sophisticated methods. A study carried out on behalf of NBC in 1927 foreshadowed the use of demographics in audience research. While these methods may have indicated what some people thought of the programmes, it did not give an accurate estimate of how many people were actually listening. The larger networks began to develop more sophisticated methods. A study carried out on behalf of NBC in 1927 foreshadowed the use of demographics in audience research; the study not only attempted to measure the size of the audience and record the days and number of hours during which they listened, but it also gathered information on the economic status of the listeners. In 1930 CBS carried out its own survey (offering a free map to all who wrote in). CBS used the information it gathered to compare responses of different counties; this led to the first CBS coverage map. None of these methods amounted to a reliable means of measuring the size of the audience.

Radio grew rapidly – between 1930 and 1935 the profits of the three networks had doubled, and this at a time when the USA was in a deep depression, but listening to the radio was cheap and although there was not a lot of money around, life went on and people still bought things. In a way this made the commercial environment even more competitive: manufactures, and it follows from that, advertisers, were chasing less money. As the audience grew so did development in research. By the end of the 1920s, Crossley Business Research Company was using the telephone as the basis of its measurement technique – people were called up and asked whether they had heard of particular programmes. Such a survey had been conducted in 1927 for a baking powder company and again, two years later for Eastman Kodak. Archibald Crossley, the founder of Crossley Business Research, produced a report for the Association of National Advertisers (ANA) *The Advertiser Looks at Radio* in which he argued the case for regular and continuous audience surveys. ANA members agreed to pay a monthly fee for such a service and in March 1930 the Cooperative Analysis of Broadcasting (CAB) began. This was the first regular ratings service. It quickly began to be referred to as the Crossley ratings and was enthusiastically followed by the popular press who charted the rise and fall of the popularity of programmes and personalities. To begin with the service was only available to advertisers; however, in 1937 NBC and CBS became subscribers. This set the pattern for the future of such organisations, reflecting the need on the part of both advertisers and broadcasters for the same kind of information.

Measuring Radio Audiences

If acquiring accurate data on television audiences is difficult enough, for radio it is even more so. Radio is more likely than television to be a 'background' medium, that is listened to while performing another activity and, aggravating the difficulty of audience measurement as the audience is frequently on the move. In the UK, radio audience for both the BBC and commercial stations is undertaken by a single company, Radio Joint Audience Research Limited (RAJAR). Established in 1992, it is wholly owned by the BBC and the Commercial Radio Companies Association (CRCA). All commercial stations with listening populations of one million or more have a minimum research sample of 1,000. Where this is not available within the quarter, the sample is built up over 6 months. Those with listening populations between 300,000 and 999,999 use 6 month samples of at least 500; those with less than 300,000 have a 12 month sample of a minimum of 300.

The BBC does something slightly different. Local/regional BBC stations in the 1.75–4 million region use a sample of 650 based on 3 months field work. Those stations with populations under 300,000 again have a sample of 650, but built up over 12 months. The basic research instrument is the diary. These are placed and collected by interviewers and completed by the respondents over a seven day period. Results for BBC and commercial national and regional stations are published on a quarterly basis.

Research Methodology

Audience measurement is continuous for all radio services throughout 50 weeks of the year, excluding the Christmas and New Year period. Diaries are customised to include the stations listened to by each respondent. Before 1998, all members of the household were interviewed, but now it is only the adults (which for the purpose of the research is anyone over 15) and up to two children. Respondents are chosen by asking all survey household members to fill in a Recruitment Questionnaire. Demographic details of the household and each member are recorded. Information on the number of radios in the households, and car radios is also recorded. One adult member is selected to maintain a dairy. Diaries are customised by asking each respondent to sort through a set of cards containing the names of all the radio stations in the area. The respondent is then asked to select:

- stations listened to or heard in the last year;

- stations heard elsewhere or chosen by somebody else;

- any other station heard in the past year.

This data is used to produce a repertoire of the respondent's radio stations, which are entered into the diary by the interviewer. There are marked similarities between the radio and television methodologies, to the point where they have virtually converged, due to developments in metering technology.

The Complete Diary

The diary has two sections: the first is a self-completion questionnaire which covers all media use including television, newspapers, Internet and radio listening via the television; the second session is used to record radio listening and covers the period from Monday to Sunday. There are two pages for each day. The day is divided into quarter-hour time segments from 6 a.m. to midnight, with midnight to 6 a.m. divided into half-hour segments. Each day starts at 4 a.m. The time segments are listed down the side of each page while the labels showing the name of the radio station appear on the fold-out flap across the page.

Whenever the radio is listened to for 5 minutes or more, respondents draw a line through the appropriate time-segment box, relevant to the 'station listened to' box. Another line is drawn through a 'where listened' column to show where the listening took place – 'at home', 'at work' 'in a car, van, lorry' or 'elsewhere'. If no listening has taken place over any half-day period, the respondent duly records this. Respondents add to the diary the name of any station that is listened to other than those selected. The diary contains details of the names, frequencies and programme content for each listed radio service. There is also a page devoted to any comments that the respondent may wish to make on stations and programmes listened to. As an incentive, there are two monthly draws: one for 4–14 year olds and another for 15–24 year olds, these age groups being the most likely to fall away from a survey.

Portable People Meter (P.P.M.)
That diary-based methods of audience research are unreliable is well known, not least because they are totally dependent on the respondents' diligence and accuracy in maintaining them. In order to go some way in overcoming these difficulties, Arbitron have developed 'The Portable People Meter', what they claim is as close to passive audience measurement as we can get. Consumers don't have to press buttons every time they start or stop watching TV. Nor do consumers have to write an entry in a paper diary every time they watch TV or listen to radio. The Portable People Meter (PPM) is about the size of the average pager and is worn by the respondent. It has the capacity to track any broadcast,

analogue or digital, whether it is carried over the air, by cable, satellite or on the Internet. There is no need for the Portable Meter to be attached to a radio receiver, as with previous metering devices; radio audiences are measured electronically.

On the face of it, the PPM is the answer to the problem of measuring radio (and indeed other media audiences), but just what is being measured? The questions raised about the nature of the television audience apply as much, perhaps even more, to radio. The nature of radio listening is often different from watching television. About the only exception to this is where house-bound individuals have the television on as 'background' in the same way that the radio may be used. Radio can be listened to far more frequently than television can be watched. Radio can be listened to just about anywhere outside the home, especially on the car and on headsets. Radio is frequently a 'secondary medium: we listen to it while doing something else' (Crisell 1986, p. 223). Most of us are probably familiar with the experience of shifting levels of attention to radio, even when listening to talk programmes. It is easy to listen to radio while engaged in other activities – indeed, for many people this is the preferred, and sometimes only way in which radio is used. Crisell provides a hypothetical account of how radio might be used:

Let us take the case of the company representative who in a typical working day travels a hundred miles from her base to visit three or four of her customers in a single town. For the two hours or so of her initial journey she can listen to her car radio without interruption, perhaps hearing two complete programmes on Radio 4. But then she arrives at her first call, and irrespective of the point which the present programme has reached, she must switch off: the day is short, there are several customers to visit, and the length of her visits will vary. Thenceforward her use of the radio will be in short snatches and at unforeseeable intervals between visits. In terms of the programmes that radio has

*traditionally provided, this use of the medium is
almost nonsensical: the programme planners would
have a headache in providing for our company 'rep'
alone, quite apart from all the other people listening
at times and for spells, which are equally arbitrary.*
(Crisell 1986, p. 214)

A good deal of radio programming seems to have
'factored in' this kind if intermittent listening. Few
programmes demand continuous listening, such as
drama or expository documentary, most others can be
'dipped' in and out of. Even single dramas can now be
listened to in an episodic fashion, over a period of time
rather than at once, thanks to Internet 'off air' facilities.
Listeners are able to access many BBC programmes on
the Internet, at the time of their choosing (see
www.bbc.co.uk/radio).

Ironically, given that virtually all other such channels are
easily listened to intermittently, it is music channels that
are potentially the least flexible, demanding the longest
periods of time from its audience. The clearest instance
of this is classical music, which accounts for more than
three quarters of Radio 3's output. When operas, longer
symphonies and plays are broadcast, a single programme
can last in excess of two hours. This is not the case with
the UK's other classical channel, Classic FM, as it does
not generally broadcast complete works. However, on
the whole it seems that the radio listener is less beholden
to the schedules than the television audience. Many
radio channels are 'themed' in that they specialise either
in talk (Radio London) or in certain kind of music (Music
FM, Jazz FM, Kiss FM, etc.). Local radio maintains a
substantial audience share across the country (both BBC
and independent) in part because of the way it links
people with their immediate area, but also through
'phone in' shows (both music and talk) that enable the
listener to feel that they have a greater investment in the
show, that they are part of it – a sense that can be
enjoyed by listeners who do not actually participate in
this way.

Listeners are also active, argues Crisell, in that they are not beholden to the schedules. This is not to say that schedules are ignored (without a schedule, that is to say ordered programming, real choice would be virtually impossible – it would become arbitrary, although with some listeners, it is). Crisell identifies a kind of tension between the free will of the listener and the structure provided by schedules:

> *The listener is undeniably active in the sense that she has no need to adjust to the daily schedules that radio provides: on the contrary, she imports it into her own daily schedule and often in a casual, fitful way – at unpredictable times and for unpredictable spells. But predictability must characterise its output, in the sense that its structure should be familiar to her and its content should accord with her tastes, and she must not be made to feel that her use of the medium is causing her to miss out on anything of great importance.*
> **(Crisell 1986, p. 216)**

The Cinema Audience

It would be reasonable to think that cinema has an almost infallible way of measuring audiences – through box office takings. But the issue of what is being measured is as problematic with cinema as it is with television. On the face of it the number of tickets sold corresponds to the number of people sitting in the audience. But that, so to speak, is only part of the story. Even though the cinema audience is regarded, by the industry anyway, as being stable (they cannot 'zap' from film to film with a remote control, are unlikely to engage in other activities or leave the room) the number of tickets sold says little. The number of people sitting in the cinema says nothing about how they responded to the film and why, or how many, will show up the next and subsequent nights. Even where information is obtained about how an audience reacts to a film, it is of limited use in predicting how the audiences will respond to another. There are some exceptions but they tend to be special cases. It is safe to predict that a James Bond film will attract an audience. The elements of a Bond film are so narrowly prescribed that they function as a series, with each film being the equivalent of an episode: an audience that liked one episode will usually anticipate enjoying the next.

'Nobody Knows What Makes a Hit'

Usually with series or sequel(s), each film is a discrete narrative. Exceptionally, this was not the case with the three *Lord of the Rings* (2001–3), where each film was a constituent episode of a single narrative. A film of such unusual length (something like 9 hours) is able to be unusually faithful to the source book, thus pleasing (and attracting) fans of the book, as well as appealing to those who had not read it. Bond and *Rings* are cases where, on the face of it, they generate their own audiences. But this is only true in a very limited way. They still have to be heavily marketed in order to maximise their box office potential, but the advantage they have over other films is that a lot is known about the *potential* audience. Even with cycles of films and sequels, there is little guarantee that an audience for one will be there for the next. Determining a future audience for a film is a tricky business and efforts to do so are often wrong. But then the economics of the industry are not predicated upon all films making money, but rather on most of them losing it with just a few making a great deal.

Commenting upon the unpredictability of audiences, economist Arthur De Vany and W. David Walls expressed a well known industry truism: 'nobody knows what makes a hit or when it will happen' (Stokes and Maltby 1999, p. 1). 'Hits' are made, they argued, 'not by revealing preferences they already have , but by discovering what they like' (ibid., p. 1). Films are not standardised products. Even with genre films, where one would expect a measure of similarity from one to the other, there are differences – there have to be: audiences are not going to see the same film over and over again.

Genre (and ultimately all narrative cinema) is about a tension between similarity and difference. As Richard Maltby writes, 'In most other acts of repeated consumption, purchasers' expectations are met exactly by a standardised product identical to those previously consumed' (ibid., p. 1). Audience behaviour, however, is shaped by the difference between viewers' expectations of any given movie before they see it and their evaluation of it afterwards. It's here that 'word of mouth' comes into play, the element of publicity that producers have little control over and that can be decisive in the success (or otherwise) of a film.

For a long time the myth held sway that the film industry, Hollywood in particular, knew little about their audience. But the reality has always been different, even if early methods were somewhat impressionistic and subjective. Hollywood producer Adolph Zukor's approach to audience research was basic to say the least. In his autobiography he described how he would visit a cinema and sit six seats from the front, watching the faces of the audience, 'turning around to do so. …With a little experience I could see, hear and "feel" the reaction to each melodrama and comedy' (ibid., p. 61). Richard Maltby argues the apparent ignorance of its audience was cultivated by Hollywood as part of a process of self-mythologisation, 'which presents multinational corporations as dream factories and helps to disguise the brute determination of the economic in the production of mass entertainment.' A 'dream factory', it would seem, is incompatible with a real factory and the '… history of movie entertainment is consequently often itself presented as a form of entertainment, and the catalogue of surprise hits, unexpected flops and moguls' intuitions constantly reinforces the industry's self-representation that show business is really no business' (ibid., p. 1).

The Emergence of Gallup

The first attempt to put cinema audience research on to a systematic basis was carried out by George Gallup in the 1930s. He had already gained substantial experience in political polling and thought that the same methods, that drew on psychological concepts, could be applied to the media. In the 1920s Gallup wrote a dissertation, funded by the publisher of *Des Moines Register*, entitled 'An Objective Method for Determining Reader Interest in the Content of a Newspaper'. In contrast to the impressionistic and subjective methods used by newspaper editors in determining what readers liked, Gallup had interviewers visit people in their homes and 'go through a copy of the paper with them, page by page, asking them to point out absolutely everything they read' (Susan Ohmer cited in ibid., p. 63). This early example of ethnographic media research led to some startling results that 'turned accepted wisdom on its head'. Gallup concluded that few people actually read the news. 'The most popular feature proved to be the picture page, followed closely by the comics. Sports columns, advice to the lovelorn and even obituaries received more attention than social and political analysis' (ibid., p. 63). 'Within six years, the annual national expenditure on comic strip advertising jumped from less than $1000 to $16.5 million... Gallup's research was understood to have revealed previously inaccessible desires among readers, and to have suggested how advertisers could reach this deeper level of consciousness by using imagery instead of words' (ibid., p. 63).

The Opinion Poll

Gallup is best known today for his work in opinion research: Gallup is synonymous with 'poll'. In fact his work in opinion research 'came directly out of market research'. His methods were highly systematic and results were presented in a 'quantitative form, using percentages, and graphs'. This approach had never been used in cinema audience research. Indeed, this was part of the attraction of working with film for Gallup – he perceived it as a methodological challenge. He had been told 'you can research politics and products and advertisements and all theses things, but … research has no place in the field of motion pictures' (ibid., p. 65). It was in 1934–5 that he began considering research in film audiences. In the summer of 1939 he approached both Darryl F. Zanuck and Louis B. Mayer, but although both were interested, they did not follow through with a contract. Zanuck and Mayer were established heads of two of the biggest Hollywood studios (20th Century Fox and MGM respectively) – it was a couple of independent producers (David O. Selznick and Sam Goldwyn) and the recently bankrupt RKO that were the first to commission audience research from Gallup. They were able to use Gallup to enhance their position as independents within the studio system. 'For RKO, hiring Gallup was a demonstration of its commitment to produce money making pictures that audiences would enjoy and thus improve its balance sheets' (Susan Ohmer cited in ibid., p. 66).

ARI and RKO

In 1940 (about the time that Gallup set up the Audience Research Institute) he signed a one year contract with RKO to undertake audience research. At the time RKO was in financial trouble: they had come out of bankruptcy only three months previously, in January. It was about that time, in the wake of the Mercury Theatre's infamous production of *The War of the Worlds*, that George Schaeffer, the president of RKO, invited the young Orson Welles down to make a film – any film. A year later the novice film-maker came up with *Citizen Kane* (1941). Gallup's task was to ascertain who the audience was, and what they wanted.

When Gallup started there was no data available that could enable him to profile audiences. He decided that one way to acquire the information he needed was to 'piggy back' his audience research onto his political poll research. From 1936 to the late 1940s he asked people who responded to his political polls about their film-going habits. The ensuing data enabled to Gallup create a detailed statistical description of the audience in terms of age, gender and class and with some sweeping generalisations that can be summarised thus:

- teenagers formed the largest film going sector (nearly one third of all tickets were purchased by people under 20 years of age);
- poor people (earning less than $15 a week and people on relief) accounted for 25% of tickets sold;
- upper middle and upper income people accounted for 15%;
- lower middle class (earning between $25–35 a week) accounted for 22%.

On this basis, it was recommended that RKO should not produce 'highbrow' films. Furthermore, Gallup's chief assistant for film research, David Ogilvy, argued, 'When films cost fortunes and distribution has only a few main channels, it is imperative that every feature should appeal to the largest possible number of theatregoers. At present there is no room for pictures which appeal to minorities' (cited in ibid, p. 70). Gallup went on to analyse the components of a film in terms of their marketing potential, recommending among other things that '...every picture carries the strongest possible title... the fact remains that a weak title always impairs box office potential, and a strong title always helps it' (cited in ibid., p. 71). ARI calculated that 25% of tickets were sold on the basis of the film's title.

It was part of the deal that ARI should provide RKO with story ideas 'that have been tested for their interest value with the motion picture public' (cited in ibid., p. 71). ARI recommend that they should use best selling novels and magazine stories 'because they had a built in audience'. ARI also researched the box office appeal of RKO's stars. ARI's research was instrumental in keeping Fred Astaire at RKO. After the failure of *Broadway Melody* (1940) RKO wanted to know if it was due to a decline in Astaire's popularity or a negative reaction to his co-star,

Eleanor Powell. ARI found that Astaire was the film's principal draw and that the public wanted to see him and Ginger Rogers back together. RKO had actually dropped Astaire in 1939 but he went on to sign another contract with the studio in July 1940. RKO announced that Astaire and Rogers would be reunited the following year in 1941.

As part of Gallup's 'upgrading' of RKO's marketing strategies, he turned his attention to the preview. In the past these had been largely industry affairs with selected audiences of largely industry insiders. Gallup maintained that such audiences did not reflect the average film-goer. Instead, he drew up preview audiences using cross-section sampling techniques to achieve 'a replica in miniature of the movie masses' (ibid., p. 74). Gallup wanted to track audience responses and so the ARI used the Hopkins Televoting Machine that had been developed for radio audience research. The Televoting Machine employed a luminous dial that the respondent could set to any of five choices – 'very dull', 'dull', 'neutral', 'like', 'like very much'. From the audience responses, a chart was produced that 'mapped', second-by-second, audience responses. Pre-production surveys and preview profiles were used to estimate a films advertising budget and the type of release pattern it was given. After some years ARI was able to claim that data from penetration studies and pre-production research could be used to predict box office receipts. Research on levels of awareness of a film could be used to calculate the amount a film was likely to make. Such information led David O. Selznick to delay the release of *Duel in the Sun* (1946) for six months, allowing it to build up its penetration level sufficiently to recoup its costs at the box office.

Gallup and ARI had put film audience research on a par with other forms of market research: techniques were evolved that, in modified form, are still used today. But this did not (and does not now) occur without criticism. Film audience research functioned 'primarily as a tool for managerial control. Producers commissioned most studies, and they strictly regulated the circulation of survey data, limiting access mainly to executives' (Susan Ohmer cited in Stokes and Maltby 2001, p. 75) The Screen Writers Guild complained that writers had to develop characters and plots according to predetermined patterns. Others complained that RKO was pandering to the lowest common denominator. 'We know what *junior* wants, and he gets it... Why not find out *what senior wants?*' (Ohmer cited in ibid., p. 75). There were complaints about the Televoting Machine. The screenwriter of *Mildred Pierce* (1945), Ranald MacDougall, pointed out that audiences could get so involved in a film that they might forget to move the dial, and thus register indifference.

The issues that were raised by Gallup's work are still relevant today. As with television audience research, it represents an attempt to bind within scientific discourse the unpredictable and varied elements of audience responses. As Susan Ohmer writes, 'The fact that ARI continually reworked its methodology suggests, however, that "scientific" research could never offer a final word on audience preferences. Although market research deploys the authority of science in an effort to control, it also to an extent recognises the power to resist prediction' (cited in ibid., p. 77).

Audience Research Methods

Sampling

The basis of all audience research is sampling. Whatever method is used, be it diaries, telephone recall or meters, it is impractical to count every member of the audience so a representative sample has to be used instead. In order to have any legitimacy a sample must comply to the following features:

- it must be random;

- all subjects within the surveyed population must have an equal chance of being included in the sample;

- the greater the size of the sample, the greater its accuracy (bigger doesn't mean better though – 200 chosen at random will not produce results twice as accurate as 100, the sample would have to be 400).

In theory, any small group chosen at random from the population to be researched (such as the television audience) will share the same characteristics as any other. In order to minimise bias, the sample must not only be randomly chosen, but each member of the population must have an equal chance of being included (a major flaw with telephone recall).

Having decided on the population (the 'universe') to be surveyed, elements or units of analysis are selected. In US TV ratings it will generally be households with TV sets; with radio it is individual listeners, the unit used in UK TV measurement. Nielsen refer to their 'populations' as Designated Market Areas (DMAs). Both in the UK and USA the buying and selling of time is done on the basis of individual populations of people defined by demographics. Audience 'populations' are usually sold in units of 1000: the larger the anticipated audience, the higher the cost of broadcast time.

A *sampling frame* is constructed, which is a list of elements to be included in the sample, ensuring that every member of the population has an equal chance of being selected. One home might be randomly selected from a list of the total population and then the process repeated until a large enough sample has been achieved. This is a simple random sample. As it is virtually impossible to compile a totally accurate list of every TV owning household, it is rarely used. Other strategies have to be employed that, while not having the full measure of statistical accuracy as simple random sampling, are good enough.

Systematic Random Sampling

This is a variation of simple sampling. The usual sampling frame is an easily obtainable list of household telephone numbers. Unlisted numbers are included through computer generated random numbers, producing an *expanded* or *total* sampling frame. The sampling then takes place, based upon a sampling interval, such as every tenth home – the sampling interval being determined by the level of statistical significance required. There is always an element of error in the actual application of this method by ratings companies, as a complete list of the population is impossible to obtain and a minority of homes will not have a telephone, while others will have more than one, giving them a greater chance of being selected.

Multistage Cluster Sampling

Multistage cluster sampling avoids the necessity of acquiring a complete list of very member of the population. It is a two-stage process, each of which has to be repeated, systematic random sampling is a one-stage process.

> *Most ratings services use this method to identify a national sample – only with great difficulty could they come up with a complete list of every household in the country. Instead, they draw up a random sample of counties. Nielsen does this to begin the process of creating a national sample. Block groups within these counties are selected and randomly sampled. Specific city blocks within selected groups are selected and randomly sampled. Finally with a manageable number of city blocks identified, researchers might be placed in the field, with specific instructions, to find individual households to participate in the sample.*
> **(Webster et al. 2000, p. 102)**

With this method a sample frame that lists every household is not required and each one can be contacted even if they do not have phones. However, there is a statistical disadvantage: in any sampling process, the chances of error increase with the number of stages.

Stratified Sampling

This is a more complex method, but has the advantage of being able to reduce error. The population being surveyed is broken down into discrete categories, called strata (which can be gender, age or anything else). Each one is then sampled. All of the samples are then put into one large group, creating a probability sample with the right proportions of men and woman, or whatever other category has been used. This improves the representative accuracy of the sample, which would otherwise be left to chance; accuracy can be further enhanced by combining stratified with multi-stage sampling.

Longitudinal Studies

Most audience measurements are cross-sectional surveys, which give a kind of 'snapshot' of a population at a particular moment in time. Longitudinal studies can describe changes in a population *over* time. There are two kinds: *trend studies* and *panel studies*.

Trend studies

Trend studies are basically cross-sectional studies, using any of the methods described above, carried out over a period of time. Although the definition of the population will remain the same throughout the study, individual members can change. A longitudinal study could simply be a succession of ratings reports, tracing a station or programme performance over time. The BARB panel is a good example of an ongoing trend study, insofar as it continuously monitors the viewing behaviour of a substantial sample group over time.

Panel Studies

Panel studies draw a sample from the population and study it continuously over a period of time, usually through a form of metering and diaries. The best example of this kind of research is the BARB panel.

However, alternative (and cheaper) methods have been employed. In 1997 the Australian government imposed substantial cuts on the Australian Broadcasting Corporation and ways were sought to reduce the research budget. Denis List came up with the idea of a phone-in panel, which was tried out at an Adelaide radio station.

The panel was recruited from an earlier random survey, each of whom were asked to provide information about their listening behaviour:

• their age group;

• their sex;

• the area where they lived ;

• their occupation type, in five broad groups;

• how much time they spent listening to the station ;

• time zones when they listened to this station; e.g.

• weekday breakfast,

• weekday morning,

• weekday afternoon,

• weekday drive,

• night,

• weekend morning,

• weekend afternoon;

• other radio stations they listened to regularly.

Each one of them was given a 3 digit serial number. Our instructions to them were:

Whenever you're listening to this station, and you hear something that you really like, dislike, or just feel like commenting on, dial our free-call number, quote your serial number (or your name, if you can't

remember the serial number), and record a message on our answering machine. Every time you leave a message, you'll be in a draw for a small prize, such as a T-shirt, or a coffee mug with the station logo.
(Dennis List,
http://www.audiencedialogue.org/case3.html)

Listeners comments were classified as positive, negative or 'other'. Once transcribed from an answer machine, they were e-mailed to the station manager and producers. Every fortnight a summary of the comments was produced, showing the number of positive, negative and 'other' comments. The system was cheap and more reliable than a conventional 'phone in':

Mainly because people who spontaneously contact a station are usually in some special position: perhaps they know somebody on the station staff, perhaps they have some axe to grind, perhaps they are just bored. Whatever the reason, it's not safe to regard them as typical listeners. The important element of this panel was the random selection. Because the participants had been originally selected at random from the whole population, we knew that (in aggregate) they had to be typical.
(Dennis List,
http://www.audiencedialogue.org/case3.html)

Numeracal accuracy was not a factor. What List and his collegues were interested in was the equivalent of BARB's satisfaction index, an indicator of what people thought of the programmes, rather than *how many* were listening.

Measurement
Measurement is 'a process of assigning numbers to objects according to rules of assignment'. The objects of audience research are either households or people. Numbers are used to quantify characteristics or behaviours under study – this simplifies managing

relevant information and summarising attributes. While it is easy to assign numbers, it is less so to make them meaningful. What kind of correspondence is there between statistical data and real audiences? At one level, advertisers are primarily concerned with audience size, and the accuracy of the numbers used to represent this. Accuracy expressed in terms of *reliability* and *validity*.

Reliability is the extent to which a procedure will repeatedly produce consistent results 'if the object of measurement does not change, an accurate measuring device should assign the same number time after time'. Reliability in itself does not mean accuracy: figures might be reliably wrong!

Validity is the extent to which a measure actually 'quantifies the characteristic under examination' (Webster et al. 2000, p.113). or the degree to which a measure corresponds to an actual state of affairs – their accuracy.

What is being measured?

There might be no interest in the audience in terms of programme content – some researchers are concerned with how much TV is watched overall. For advertisers, however, this is of little concern as they are interested in exposure only insofar as it is tied to specific programmes. There is the question of what constitutes 'exposure', especially with current technology that can provide viewing every ten seconds. There is also the issue of what is meant by 'exposure'. The industry has a fairly minimum definition, the only thing relevant being who is present when the TV is in use. It has been found, however, that presence in a room when the television is switched on does not necessarily count as exposure to whatever is being broadcast. We all know from our own experience, and this has been confirmed by researchers as being very widespread, that audiences might not be watching television at all, but be engaged in a host of unrelated activities. There is, then, the question of *quality* of exposure. It is almost certainly the case that industry researchers constantly over-estimate real exposure time, if we mean by exposure the act of viewing television with a sufficient level of concentration to be aware of what is being transmitted. Even the most sophisticated peoplemeter cannot 'measure' the degree of involvement any member of the audience has with the screen.

The 'Holy Grail' of audience of measurement is to find a method that is totally independent of the audience. Diary techniques have long been regarded as the most unreliable as they are totally dependent on people bothering to keep them up to date. Given that the peoplemeter has to be manually operated, it attracts little more confidence than the diary. The proliferation of satellite, cable and digital channels has exacerbated the problem:

It used to be easy. You watched M*A*S*H on Monday night and you'd put that in the diary. Now if you have thirty channels on cable you watch one channel, switch to a movie, watch a little MTV, then another program, and the next morning with all that switching all over the place you can't remember what you've watched.
(David Poltrack, vice president of research for CBS, cited in Ang 1996, p. 72)

Even with the best intentioned audience member, unless viewing data is entered immediately, as likely as not, it will be inaccurately recalled. Rapid and frequent channel switching has made the diary obsolete. The goal has been to develop a passive meter that does not require any intervention on the part of the audience, the efficacy of which cannot be undermined by its capricious behaviour.

Scheduling Methods and Programme Choice

Television is a highly competitive industry. It is the aim of all broadcasters to achieve and maintain the largest possible audience. One way to maximise audiences is to manipulate the flow of programmes. In order to do this they have to take into account not only the merits of each individual programme available for transmission, but also what is known of the programming of competing broadcasters. It's not enough to capture an audience for one programme; the audience must be maintained across the evening, each day of the week. What broadcasters seek to do is to assemble a package of programmes and arrange the order of their transmission in such a way as to keep the largest possible audience all evening, across the week. Raymond Williams described this as programme 'flow' (Williams 1974, pp. 72-112). By flow Williams intended to convey a sense of a seamless stream of programmes designed to 'lock' the audience in for a whole evening. Traditional scheduling was all about creating a sense of channel loyalty where the audience would watch the one channel for most, if not all, the evening, every evening.

Now that digital, cable and satellite have expanded the number of channels, traditional scheduling methods are less effective than they were. The real blow to schedulers was not cable, digital or satellite, but something far more modest: the remote control. We all know how easy 'channel hopping' is – the moment we no longer had to walk half way across the room to 'turn over', channel loyalty and programme flow were doomed.

Another blow to traditional scheduling methods was the video recorder, enabling the audience to 'time shift', that is to record, and later watch, any programme at a time of their choosing. For broadcasters and advertisers the most alarming aspect of 'time shifting' is the concomitant practice of 'fast-forwarding' – or 'zipping' – through the commercials. Although the primary commercial function of broadcasters is to deliver to advertisers audiences who are watching their advertisements, there is evidence suggesting that this is not happening on the scale indicated by even the most sophisticated audience measuring methods: even when there is an audience in front of the television set, the viewers are not necessarily paying any attention.

TiVo

TiVo is the latest nightmare for schedulers and advertisers. It is a tapeless VCR that digitally records up to 80 hours of television programmes, saving them onto a hard drive. The user is able to programme TiVo with his/her programme preferences using a remote called Thumbs Up. 'Thumbs Up' refers to the Thumbs Up and Thumbs Down button used to rate programmes, whether live or pre-recorded. The TiVo DVR builds up a sense of the user's programme preferences. Information on what programmes are available are automatically downloaded to the TiVo DVR. Digital recording devices such as TiVo are not only able to record many hours of programmes, but they can be set to automatically record complete series of programmes. Facilities such as TiVo's WishList can be programmed to record any material that matches the user's interests: it can then be watched or deleted at any time. Although still in its infancy, some systems have the ability to skip advertising altogether by automatically recognising the beginning and end of programmes. In any case, adverts can be zipped through in a matter of seconds. The head of the FCC in the US, Michael Powell, who himself owns a TiVo said, 'This is God's machine'. Owners of such technology need never see an advert again. Not only is advertising avoided, but so are the broadcasters' carefully planned schedules, which are rendered redundant.

Themes and 'stripping'

Other scheduling methods have been introduced to try to capture the audience, such as 'themes' and 'stripping'. 'Themes' are used by all of the terrestrial broadcasters. The whole of an evening, or a substantial part of it, is devoted to a single programme theme which might be a genre, the work of an actor, director or other subject. To enhance the chances of retaining the audience, there will sometimes be an 'anchoring' device that punctuates the whole evening. This might be an interview, or series of interviews. In the case of BBC's NHS day in 2001, a series of programmes and items were punctuated by returning to the hospital from which the evening was being anchored. From time-to-time, themes will be 'stripped' across a weekend. This is where episodes of the same programme are broadcast each night across the week or weekend.

Until 1954 the BBC was the only UK broadcaster. With the arrival of independent television, an element of competition set in. But the degree of this competition, compared to what it is today, was minimal. Both broadcasters, on the whole, provided different but complementary programming. The BBC had a public broadcaster remit to fulfil; ITV, less constrained, was able to provide more populist fare, although they too had to fulfil certain PSB requirements. It was a model that worked well, because although the BBC and ITV were in competition for audiences, they were not in competition for revenue, the BBC being funded by the licence fee and ITV through advertising. It was also only up to a point that they were in competition for the audience. ITV, with its more populist approach to programming would invariably capture the larger slice of the audience, but this did not matter too much to the BBC so long as they could maintain a large enough number in order to justify the licence fee. So long as most people watched some BBC some of the time, it did not matter if they had the smaller audience so long as they were seen to be fulfilling their PSB remit (an issue very much alive as the BBC heads for its 2006 Charter review).

This proved to be to their advantage when in 1960 the Pilkington Committee was convened to decide who should have the third television channel, the BBC or ITV. The Pilkington Committee was concerned with what it regarded as the triviality of ITV programming and the BBC won the new channel, which became BBC2. ITV had to wait until 1980 before another commercial channel came on stream, Channel 4. But C4 was a channel with a difference, a sort of commercial BBC2, tasked with the mission of providing 'alternative' programming.

Until the 1980s, the terrestrial broadcasters in the UK, the BBC and ITV (C4 was largely funded by ITV), had only each other to worry about and were both able to employ a fairly straightforward scheduling strategy, based on some well understood tactics:

• inheritance;

• hammocking;

• pre-echo;

• pre-scheduling.

Inheritance
Inheritance is the placing of either a new programme or one of less obvious appeal to a large audience after a popular programme. The assumption, or hope, is that some of the audience will stay with the new programme rather than change channel.

Hammocking

A 'weak' programme, or one that is either new or of minority interest, is placed in between two popular programmes. This is a surer way of maintaining an audience for a new or minority interest programme than 'inheritance'.

Pre-echo

A 'weak' programme is placed before a popular programme. The assumption is that some of the audience for the popular programme will tune in early and see at least some of the preceding programme.

Pre-scheduling

The regional structure of ITV, with its network of separate companies, had in the past made scheduling more problematic for ITV than the BBC. This is now less so as scheduling for ITV is now done centrally through Network Central. ITV is also much less a patchwork of autonomous companies than it used to be, as ownership itself has largely become concentrated into two companies, Central and Granada (the merger of the two companies – creating a single company called ITV plc – was sanctioned by the UK Government in October 2003). With more channels, audiences become more fragmented, a process that has been continuing since the 1980s that saw the arrival of C4 at the beginning of the decade, followed by the expansion of cable and then satellite, which became dominated by Rupert Murdoch's Sky.

Cinema Audience Testing

The standard methods used today include:

- previews;
- marketing previewing;
- audience tracking.

Previews

The preview is a long established means of testing a film on an audience: it was a feature of the Hollywood studio system even its early days. NRG, a subsidiary of Neilson Research, is the leading 'player' in cinema audience testing. They charge between $10,000–$20,000 per preview screening; on average, a studio release will have nine previews (*Screen International,* 23 November 2001). The standard way of organising a preview is to canvass the public, usually in a shopping area, and invite them to see a film. Sometimes the invitation will be reinforced with information such as the name of the director, star, genre, etc. Usually a group of about 150 people is gathered together at a nearby cinema. Of these, about 20 will be asked to participate in a post-screening focus group. All of the 150 are given comment cards with questions such as 'Did you like this film?' The respondent is asked to fill in one of five boxes, with answers ranging from 'love' to 'hate'. Information is also requested regarding age and gender.

The focus group is asked more detailed questions about aspects of the plot and their responses to them. NRG tabulates the results against normative data that NRG has established for different genres.

Marketing Previewing

Marketing previewing is where the constituent elements of a marketing campaign, such as trailers and posters, are tested on audiences. The methodology for testing trailers is similar to that used with films, except that they are usually tried out on both sample audience and individuals who then have to complete a questionnaire. Smaller locations are sometimes used (I was once invited into a pub in Woolwich to watch a couple of trailers for a Bond film).

Audience Tracking

Audience tracking is used to assess the extent of public awareness of a film. Members of the public are polled by telephone and asked if they recognise the film's title, whether they have seen it or intend

to see it: telephone polling has been supplemented by the Internet. On-line ticketing services such as MovieTickets.com and Moviefone in the USA and Odeon in the UK are able to gather information on who wants to see a particular film through on-line advance bookings. Fandango sold more than 500,000 Harry Potter tickets in North America in advance of its release, representing 4% of the movie's estimated weekend tally.
(Screen International, 23 November 2001, p. 7)

Aspects of Consumption

Minority Audiences

Fans and Audience Research

Evidence of the ways in which audiences can not only be 'active' in terms of making meaning, but also engaging creatively with texts and reinventing them has emerged through a number of studies of 'fandom'. Henry Jenkins writes in *Textual Poachers* (1992) the 'fan' has more often than not been regarded with some derision. 'Fan' is an abbreviation of 'fanatic', which itself is derived from the Latin 'fanaticus', meaning 'of or belonging to the temple, a temple servant, a devotee...: of persons inspired by orgiastic rites and enthusiastic frenzy'. It is the 'enthusiastic frenzy' part of the definition that is retained in contemporary usage, along with 'any excessive and mistaken enthusiasm' (Jenkins 1992, p.12). Fans are often seen as fanatics and deranged (ibid.). Lewis (1992) defines 'fans' as a set of devoted followers of a star or text. 'Fandom', McQuail (1997) writes, 'is often associated in the view of critics with immaturity and mindlessness, an outcome of mass culture and an example of mass behaviour.'

Jenkins (1992) argues that two models of the 'pathological fan' has emerged. There is the 'obsessed loner' who has entered into an imagined, fantasy relationship with a celebrity. In extreme cases, the 'fan' will stalk, threaten – or worse – the object of their devotion. Such an example – thankfully rare – is Mark Chapman who killed John Lennon. The second model is that of the 'frenzied or hysterical member of a crowd'

(Jenkins 1992, p. 11). Other derogatory archetypes are boozy, racist football fans and screaming fans at pop concerts. Within the high-culture mind-set, these images are the distillation of all that is bad about the 'fan'.

It is significant, in my view, that the term 'fan' is generally applied to devotees of popular culture. There are no 'opera fans', for example, but there are opera 'buffs', a term implying knowledge and expertise rather than being either a 'victim' of media exploitation or a mindless obsession. An enthusiasm for 'high culture' – music, theatre, literature – would generally be regarded as worthy, testament to the education, taste and cultivation of the enthusiast. Not so the devotee of a television series. In reality, an amused follower of *Only Fools and Horses* could well be passionate about *The Marriage of Figaro*. While it is true that a rise in fandom has been stimulated by the media themselves through (especially in the case of films) the sale of spin-offs – games, clothes, even food labelling – all helping to extend the life of a product, increase audiences and, of course, profits, there has emerged over recent years a different view of fandom, one that empathises not passivity or vulnerability, but creativity and the construction of identities. Henry Jenkins characterises fandom as:

A cultural community, one which shares a common mode of reception, a common set of critical categories and practices, a tradition of aesthetic production, a set of social norms and expectations. I look upon fans as possessing certain knowledge competency in the area of popular cultural that is different from that possessed by academic critics and from that possessed by the 'normal' or average viewer.
(Jenkins 1992, p. 86)

These studies (by Camille Bacon-Smith (1992) and Henry Jenkins (1992)) demonstrate how fans are 'active' in the sense of creating their own meanings, but also appropriate the texts and make them their own: some groups of fans do not restrict their activities to watching and discussing their favourite programmes, but will also, either collectively or individually, re-write plots and create new ones which are shared at group meetings and printed and distributed, a process rendered easy by DTP technology or, increasingly, online. In the case of soaps, alternative actions to those devised by the scriptwriters will be invented for established characters and new characters will be invented. This will, on occasion, bring fans into conflict with producers where characters behave, or have a fate meted out to them, that is unacceptable to the fans – as with *Crossroads* and *Star Trek*.

Star Trek
Bacon-Smith identifies four types of fans' writing about *Star Trek*:

1 'Mary Sue': this is the introduction of a young woman into the Enterprise who will save the ship and crew from disaster, but dies in the process It seems this is often the first story written by the putative fan – it is, however, a disliked form and the term 'Mary Sue' is often endowed with pejorative connotations.

2 'Lay Spock' (or any other crew member): this is a story which situates Spock in a heterosexual relationship.

3 'K/S' or 'slash' – this story puts Spock in a homosexual relationship.

4 'Hurt/Comfort' – this places two characters in a close relationship, one of whom is hurt in some way and has to be cared for by the other.

An important feature of these stories is that are created collectively (Abercrombie and Longhurst 1998). A story may be initiated by one of the group, but others will become involved in a shared effort, creating an alternative *Star Trek* universe, taking the characters to where they want them to go: such story 'production goes against the stereotype of the lone author at work in creating for an industrialised book market' (ibid.). It also goes against the stereotype of the lonely, socially isolated fan. Fans' creative engagement with such programmes as *Star Trek* incorporate other activities aside from writing, such as video production and painting (see Alasuutari 1999).

Jenkins describes five ways in which fans engage with their chosen texts and 'fan culture':

- Mode of reception. Fans have a mode of reception which Jenkins characterises as 'emotional proximity and critical distance'. Fans may very well be enthusiastic about the object of their attention, often accompanied by a powerful emotional investment, but this does not mean that they abandon critical detachment.

- Viewer activism. Fans can have a 'particular set of critical and interpretative practices'. They can be active as critics, contradicting the critically passive persona frequently ascribed to them. Jenkins found that fans regularly generate their own canon – publishing and revising lists of greatest and worst ever episodes in fan magazines.

- Interpretative communities. Newcomers will be inducted into the interpretative practices of the group, in some cases virtually being tutored by a leading and experienced member. There is a self-conscious articulation of an aesthetic in the discourse of fans embracing 'continuity' and 'structure'. Skills and competencies are shared.

- Cultural production. Fans will evolve their own versions of the series, what Jenkins calls 'writing in the margins', 'creating alternative texts, placing characters from establishes series into new situations and new universes' (p. 127).

- Alternative social communities. Fans frequently create an 'alternative social community'. Groups of fans can form around such programmes as *Blake's 7* and *Star Trek* that become effective communities into which newcomers have to be inducted into the procedures by which texts are consumed, read and worked upon. Bacon-Smith explores these processes in some detail in her account of *Star Trek* fans. They not only form their own small groups, meeting to watch and discuss episodes, but also engage in larger scale social activities such as conventions.

A Sense of Identity

Leaving aside the psychopathic edge of fandom, where an exclusive obsession may give cause for concern, there is plenty of evidence from a number of studies that fandom 'underlines the potential for media experience to form the basis of distinctive subcultures and identities'. This has sometimes induced conflict between audiences and institutions. Henry Jenkins (1992) has written about one such conflict between the gay community and Paramount, the makers of *Star Trek*. An organisation for gay, lesbian and bisexual science fiction fans called Gaylactic Network Inc. has for sometime been lobbying Paramount to introduce gay characters in *Star Trek*. Gene Roddenberry (the creator of the series) went along with this request, but Paramount never followed through, other than featuring 'two episodes which can loosely be read as presenting images of alternative sexuality, *The Host* and *The Outcast*. Although the producers have promoted these stories as responsive to the gay and lesbian community's concerns, both treat queer lifestyles as alien rather than familiar aspects of the federation culture and have sparked further controversy among the Gaylaxians' (Jenkins 1992, p. 172). Jenkins writes that the 'fans requests are relatively straightforward – perhaps showing two male crew members holding hands in the ship's bar, perhaps a passing reference to a lesbian lover, some evidence that gays, bisexuals and lesbians exist in the twenty-fourth century represented on the programme.' (ibid.).

Paramount attempted to dismiss the letter writing campaign that ensued as an attempt by an 'outside influence' and 'special interest group' to interfere with the programme. The people involved in the campaign saw things rather differently. 'They saw themselves as vitally involved with the life of the series and firmly committed to its survival.' In their attempt to win over Roddenberry, they cited his successful attempt 'to get a black woman on the Enterprise bridge and his unsuccessful one to have a female second-in-command', and wondered aloud 'why can't *Star Trek* be as controversial in educating people about our movement as they were for the black civil rights movement?' (ibid., p. 174). Gay *Star Trek* fans were passionate about the campaign and 'the producers' refusal to represent gay and lesbian characters cut deeply.

> *They betrayed everything* Star Trek *was – the vision of humanity I have held for over 25 years. They betrayed Gene Roddenberry and his vision and all the fans. They didn't have the guts to live up to what* Star Trek *was for.*
> **(ibid., p. 174)**

Dyer's 'Utopia'
In his examination of why these fans felt so strongly, Jenkins draws on Richard Dyer's 'utopia' thesis. In an early exposition of his 'utopia theory' Dyer examined the Hollywood musical (Dyer, 1977), arguing that one of the pleasures of the musical is the way it constructs for the audience utopian 'worlds', although not in the sense of Sir Thomas Moore or William Morris – rather, the utopianism is contained in the feelings it embodies (see also *Making Things Perfectly* (Dyer, 1993)). It presents what utopia would feel like rather than how it would be organised. Some of Jenkins respondents in his research on Star Trek clearly articulate this 'utopian sensibility':

> *I wasn't very happy with my world as it was and found that by reading science fiction or fantasy, it took me to places where things were possible,*

things that couldn't happen in my normal, everyday life. It would make it possible to go out and change things that I hated about my life, the world in general, into something more comfortable for me, something that would allow me to become what I really wanted to be .... Being able to work out prejudices in different ways. Dealing with man's inhumanity to man. To have a vision for a future or to escape and revel in glory deeds that have no real mundane purpose. To be what you are and greater than the world around you lets you.
(ibid., p. 175)

Jenkins argues that this is 'something more than an abstract notion of escapism', that such utopian fantasies can 'provide an important first step towards political awareness, since utopianism allows us to envision an alternative social order which we must work to realise .... and to recognise the limitations of our current situation (the dystopian present against which utopian entertainment can be read)' (ibid., p. 175). Jenkins also found that Gaylaxians, through oppositional readings, interpretatively appropriated *Star Trek* and made it their own, reading into characters and situations gay traits that were not 'inscribed' by the programme's 'authors'. John Hartley, who is also a member of the Gaylaxians, has advocated a policy of 'intervention analysis' which 'needs to take popular television more or less as it finds it, without high-culture fastidiousness or right-on political squeamishness, but it needs to intervene in the media and in the production of popular knowledge *about* them' (ibid., p. 173). Sharing this position, Jenkins writes:

Such an approach may provide one way of reconciling critical work on texts, institutional analysis of the production process, and audience research on reception contexts within television studies. Rather than reading the audience from the text, an approach characteristic of ideological criticism, we should rather move to read the text from the specific perspective of particular audiences
(ibid., p.173)

There are some pertinent criticisms of the kind of research that Jenkins' has engaged in (and ethnographic research in general); that, for example, its conclusions are predicated on the duplicity of personal memory, distorted self-image on the part of the subject, and even some of the problems that confounded some effects research. Ethnographic work is vulnerable to the same experimental 'trip wires' as effect studies. These include 'experimenter expectancy bias', whereby results are interpreted in line with what was expected and the 'good subject effect', where the subject, wittingly or otherwise, conforms to the 'demand characteristics of the experimental situation' – in other words, s/he will tell the researcher what s/he expects (or wants) to hear. Not withstanding all of that, there has to be a place in audience research for what audiences themselves say about their own experiences of watching, listening and reading.

The most consistent finding of this kind of research is that readers/audiences are not held in thrall to any kind of dominant reading. Once a text is released into the world, the world will make of it what it will. Much ethnographic work has been based around audiences that have, in one way or another, been in opposition to dominant culture. Jenkins' work on gays and *Star Trek* is one instance of this.

Cultural Readings of Texts

Two interesting studies that illustrate that audiences appropriate texts in a way that makes sense in terms of their own experiences are Jhally and Lewis' work on *The Cosby Show* and Jacqueline Bobo on the film *The Color Purple* (1985).

Working with black focus groups, Jhally and Lewis found that characters depicted as poor working class were perceived negatively. The belief was that such images merely reinforced demeaning stereotypes, even if many of them were socially 'realistic', in the sense that a black person was more likely to be poor and working class than otherwise. On the other hand, one might have imagined (as people have done) that the *The Cosby Show* might also be unpopular with many black people on the grounds that it gives a grossly misleading view of the lives of black people in the USA. Jhally and Lewis, however, found that most of the black viewers they talked to had a different view of the programme. Responses included:

> It's not just a typical – being stereotyped as having only this kind of an interest or going out and partying or you know, loud music or drinking or whatever

> I admire him. I like his show because it depicts black people in a positive way. I think he's good. It's good to see that blacks can be professionals.

> That it was a black, clean show and comedy. I like comedy and … it didn't have us acting so stereotype, you know.

However, there was a price to be paid for the enjoyment of watching a non-stereotyped image of a black person, then relatively unusual in a sit-com. *The Cosby Show* was acceptable because he was rich, successful and middle class: 'Cosby's apparent move to a TV world beyond the confines of stereotyping is dependent upon the Huxtables' lofty class status as "intelligent black professionals". Without that status, the show would be seen as sliding back into the negative territory occupied by more traditional black sitcoms' (p. 260). Jhally and Lewis argue that whether or not *The Cosby Show* is typical of a real black family is 'secondary to its power to promote positive images of black life. If the display of wealth is a necessary part of it, so be it' (ibid., p. 281). Jhally and Lewis argue that in endorsing Cosby they are accepting the values of the show.

The Cosby Show may not be real, Jhally and Lewis write, 'but it is a necessary illusion'. As one of the respondents remarked:

> *I've watched talk shows where black people made adverse comments about it, I mean blacks even made adverse comments, like our children. They say it's not typical. A typical black family. Where you gonna find a lawyer and people dressed like that .... It's just a part of life ... the way things are; but I view this as clean and wholesome .... In fact I'd say it's not stereotype, you know, in the negative sort of way that makes it black female, or black male view of downtrod or suppressed.*
> **(ibid., p. 281)**

Jhally and Lewis argue that the problem with such programmes is that they place black people in an ideological double bind. On the one hand , *The Cosby Show* promotes the illusion that black people 'can make it in a predominantly white world, even though most black people have, on this reckoning, failed; second, it cultivates the illusion that economic success is achievable for black people as for white people' (ibid., p. 286).

There have been attempts to replicate the success of the *The Cosby Show* with sitcoms such as *The Fresh Prince of Bel Air*, another show that has achieved a measure of popularity in the UK. Writing from the vantage point of 2004, it is questionable whether programmes like *The Cosby Show* have such an ideological negative role as suggested by Jhally and Lewis. It's now ten years since they wrote their piece. Much appears to have changed in that time. There are far more prominent black people at all levels of American (and indeed British) society. For the first time in the USA there has been a black Secretary of State (Colin Powell) and National Security Advisor, the latter being a black woman (Condoleeza Rice). Black people have a far higher public profile, both in the USA and the UK, than before the 1990s, and this has been reflected on TV and cinema screens, including a black US President in *24*. It may well be that rather than succumbing to illusory ideological representations, audiences are well aware of the difference between image and reality.

Audience Participation

Live Audiences

It has always been thought, by television companies, that having a show with a live audience would increase the appeal for the television audience. The traditional thinking about this was that the audience at home would feel detached from the programme itself. This is not only avoided, but the reverse effect is achieved whereby the home audience is encouraged to feel that they too are part of the programme. The dynamics of the programme work to create the illusion of a community. The signifiers of the 'live' audience (applause, visual cutaways to the audience and so on) act as a guarantee of immediacy; this will work even if the programme is not being transmitted live or a time-shifted recording is being watched. The viewing audience is drawn into the programme through the use of direct address, along with the frequent use of close-ups of both presenter and participants, often looking directly at the camera. The presenters of such programmes are careful to address both the studio and home audience, reinforcing the latter's sense of belonging. The illusionary sense of a community that is created is the result of careful manipulation of all the elements of the programme, not least the audience itself, irrespective of the kind of programme, whether it is sitcom, a chat show such as *Parkinson* or a confessional talk show such as *Trisha*. Programmes that have studio audiences tend to fall into the following categories:

- sitcoms;

- stand-up comedy;

- interviews;

- talk shows;
- confessional talk shows;
- some music shows.

Of these, the confessional talk show makes the greatest use of the audience: for these programmes the audience is a crucial, even a defining element. Shows such as Trisha are structured around an audience who play an active part in the programme, contributing to discussions, making comments, posing questions and passing judgement on the participants. They can be very 'robust', to the extent that one does wonder what induces people to participate. But that is the whole point – they do, and seemingly willingly so. It must have something to do with the allure of appearing on television, but also with the nature of the programmes themselves.

The Talk Show

As a demonstration of the constructed nature of television, there is none better than a talk show. The studios tend to be small, as indeed is the 'audience'. With an effective presenter an atmosphere of intimacy is readily achieved and people will talk. The audience itself, as for all TV programmes, is manipulated. The usual relationship between audience and performer is, to a degree, inverted. To begin with the television studio audiences are beholden to the programme, because they have been given free tickets. On arrival, having been seated, they will be 'warmed up'. The producer, director or a 'warm up comic' will 'work the audience' into the appropriate mood. If, during the recording, there is not enough laughter or applause, they will be instructed to do try harder. It has to be said that the manipulation only goes so far – an audience will not be asked to entirely simulate a response. There are technical reasons why an audience will be asked to repeat a reaction, whether it be clapping or laughing, but, be that as it may, it is not quite the same thing as sitting in a theatre. Above all else, the audience is being directed by the performer/presenter – as indeed are the participants. It is this that detracts from the claim that such shows are in some way 'democratic', that they efface the hierarchy of television producer–consumer and in so doing empower and give a voice to the 'ordinary person'. Various writers have made this claim (Camille Paglia, Patricia Priest, Sonia Livingstone and Peter Lunt, and Paolo Carpignano to name but a few). In a limited way they do, but it is always within limits set by the producers. To begin with the people who appear are carefully selected and it is the presenter who sets the agenda and directs the exchanges between participants and audience. If anything, rather than being challenged, the hierarchy of television producer/audience is reasserted.

Reality Television: Reconstructing Real Events

Nothing New

'Reality TV' is a new name for an old phenomenon – documenting 'the real' on camera. It goes back to the dawn of cinema: all but one of the short films screened by August and Louis Lumière in December of 1895 in the Grande Café, Paris, were 'actualities': filmed representations of events as they unfolded before the camera – precursors of observational documentary. It was to be some time before film evolved fictional forms: for a while, film was little more than an extension of photography, borrowing its aesthetic, which itself had been derived from nineteenth century portraiture and landscape painting. 'Actualities' were little more than animated photographs.

Even these rudimentary 'documentaries', however, were fundamentally different from the kind of televisual text that is generally recognised by the term 'reality television': what was being recorded by Lumière was not a totally artificial production created from beginning to end solely for the camera. They are recognisably authentic events, representative of the real (if not real themselves). Reality TV, is however, the apotheosis of postmodernism, it is divorced from any recognisable anterior reality, totally absorbed within an artificial and abstract socio-televisual discourse. Even seemingly 'real' locations, such as the island in *Survivor,* are rendered with the same degree of artificial construction as the set of *Big Brother.* The difference between documentary and reality television, is that with the former there is an autonomous pro-filmic event (notwithstanding how it is discursively realised as film); with reality television there is no such pro-filmic event – the text is the event. It has no other existence outside the text itself. In this sense it is pure fiction, with the same ontological status as a game show, with which reality TV actually shares many features.

This is as true of historically-based reality TV, such as *The 1900s House, The 1940s House* and *The Trench.* Part of the attraction of these shows for audiences is watching people behave in unusual circumstances and seeing if they will last out the series. The only difference between *The Trench* and *Survivor* is that the latter is overtly competitive with a substantial prize awarded to the winner. They both fulfil the definition of reality TV offered by Dolan Cummings (2002): '... programmes that feature members of the public in unusual situations, often competing for a prize, and often involving audience participation'.

A Real Hybrid

Reality TV seems to have grown almost seamlessly from a form of observational documentary that became popular in the 1990s. *Driving School* and *The Cruise* spawned a multitude of successors on both sides of the Atlantic. It's easy to see how reality TV grew out of them. They were all based around ordinary people in mostly unusual situations – or, in some cases (e.g. *Driving School*) unusual people in ordinary situations. 'Reality television' is probably the most confused and confusing programming category of them all. I am deliberately resisting the term 'genre', because as a piece of language its terms of reference of 'Reality TV' are too broad – it embraces fiction and non-fiction, light entertainment and serious documentary. As a term it is indiscriminately fired off like a semantic shotgun, scattering its blast across the spectrum of television schedules. For the purposes of analysis it is virtually meaningless, connoting only that living people (well, usually living) have been placed in front of the camera. On the one hand, Gray Cavender and Mark Fishman, in their book *Entertaining Crime* (1998) use it to describe crime programmes that 'claim to present true stories about crime, criminals and victims' (p. 3). On the other hand, the term is also used to describe a programme that bundles a bunch of strangers into a confined multi-camera studio for the purposes of an elaborate 'beauty contest' where the audience weekly votes off a contestant. Yes, *contestant* – although usually described as 'reality TV' *Big Brother* is as much a game show as *Countdown*.

Reality television has at least three strands: documentary, game shows and web surveillance programmes. Its origins are in documentary with its roots buried somewhere in the early 1990s when a particular form of television observation documentary became popular and, for a time, as pervasive as 'reality game shows' are now. Observational documentaries have a long antecedence. The 1906 documentary, *A Day in the Life of a Coal Miner* is, for all intents and purposes, an observational film chronicling what the title says – a day in the life of a coal miner (or rather mine: the eponymous miner only appears at the beginning and end – leaving and returning home). Better known perhaps, there is Robert Flaherty's *Nanook of the North* (1922) which has elements of an observational documentary – recording events as they unfold in front of the camera. It also bears an intimation of the debates cum scandals that would revisit observational documentary in the 80s and 90s – Flaherty 'cheated'. There is a sequence in the film showing Nanook building an igloo: he did not, however, live in an igloo and had no idea how to build one. It was mostly built for him.

The form became popularised in the 1960s in the US by the Drew Associates: it was then called 'direct cinema'. In France it was known as *cinema verité*. Its leading practitioner was Jean Rouch. The imperative behind Drew, Leacock, etc., in films such as *Primary* (1960) was to record reality in as unmediated way as possible; Rouch realised that this aim was impossible and in films such as *A Chronicle of a Summer* (1960), made with Edgar Morin, he incorporated into his films, markers of their own production (acknowledgment of the camera and so on) – in Nichols' terms they are reflexive documentaries. In the end, the debate about how far such films can reflect or represent the real is sterile – it is an intellectual *cul de sac*; we all know that language can only construct a representation of reality, but does this invalidate documentary as a means of apprehending the world? If so, why take any kind of text seriously, written or filmic, whether it be historical, scientific or whatever? Is the film documentary to be singled out as being peculiarly resistant to the 'truth'?

Ordinary People: The Docusoap

By the 1990s the observational film had 'morphed' into the docusoap. These were observational films such as *The Cruise, Hotel, Airport*, etc., that were presented as a series. Insofar as they maintained, across a number of episodes, a continuity of character, location and narrative, they had elements of the soap opera. For a while they were popular and consequently omnipresent: all the channels were 'at it'. They even threw up their own 'stars', as short lived, it should be added, as those from 'Reality' shows. Some of these programmes ran into trouble and in so doing focused attention on the artificial nature of the enterprise. Several programme makers were caught cheating. Not only programme makers, but also participants, indulged in 'spicing up' reality to make it more 'sexy' (e.g. Flaherty). *Daddy's Girl* was ostensibly about an unusually intimate relationship between a father and daughter, but unbeknown to the programme makers, they were not related at all: they were just boy and girl friend. It seems they perpetuated the hoax in part for money, but also for the kudos of appearing on TV. In the case of *Daddy's Girl* the programme makers were duped, but it became clear that others were conspiring with 'ordinary people' appearing in the programmes to 'spice up' reality. One episode of *Builders* featured a fairly abrasive complainant who, so it turned out, was nothing of the kind and had simply acted the part.

As we have seen, one of the impulses behind reality TV is to make television more accessible (see Victoria Mapplebeck in Cummings 2002, p. 27 and Andrejevic 2004, p. 2). In *Reality TV*, Mapplebeck describes one of her own productions that was designed from the outset to converge web and television technologies, in her view opening up access more than conventional television is able. *Smart Hearts* was a five part documentary that incorporated online web access featuring the lives of a couple, Brendan Quick and Claire de Jong. The programme was transmitted by C4 and was one of their earliest 'forays into reality television'. Aside from being shown on C4, Quick and de Jong's home was equipped with several webcams: there was round-the-clock, 24 hour audience access. Mapplebeck makes the point that they had final editorial control (it was a condition they insisted upon) and they were able to turn off the webcams (as they did) whenever they wanted. In writing about this programme, Mapplebeck trots out the word 'access' like a mantra, but at no time explains the value or meaning of this access. At a superficial level such 'access' is of two kinds: on the one hand, 'ordinary people' have gained access to what is usually a very 'top-down' medium, and on the other hand, audiences are free to 'look' whenever they so choose. But the question overhanging this 'access' is so what? What is to be learned from such relatively unmediated scrutiny of others' lives, beyond a certain kind of voyeuristic pleasure?

Mapplebeck claims (Cummings p. 23) that the '…starting point for Reality TV is that the world has changed. Traditional documentary has on the whole failed to reflect these changes. The emphasis of Reality TV is unashamedly on the personal, on ethics rather than politics.' Leaving aside the astonishingly reductive and sweeping hyperbole (are all documentaries the same?), some obvious questions are begged by this – such as what kind of changes has documentary failed to reflect and how are these same changes being explored by such reality TV programmes as *Smart Hearts?*

Are We All Voyeurs?

Given the apparent rejection of any notion of 'shaping' reality, reality is presumably left free to express itself. But where does that leave the audience? How are they to make sense of these seemingly random moments of 'unmediated' bits of reality? What basis of knowledge is reality television predicated on? As Clay Calvert put it, 'Discussion is replaced by watching. Indeed the flipside of the death of discourse is …the birth of voyeurism' (Cummings p. 22). The philosophical and ethical claims for reality TV generally sound hollow: in television terms it seems to be entirely commercially led. The programmes are generally cheap to make and the form seems to have developed the capacity to endlessly reproduce itself through only marginal modifications. In fact a simple genealogy of reality TV seems already to have established itself. A new or modified idea is developed and cast with members of the public. After a series or two, the series is slightly modified having a 'celebrity special' (e.g. *Celebrity Big Brother*). The 'celebrities' concerned generally share the distinction of either being relatively unknown or hoping to invigorate their fading careers.

Proliferation and competition for audiences have encouraged ever more controversial premises for programmes. At the time of writing, there is in the US a reality TV show where female contestants are competing for a role in a porn film. Another, *The Will*, is seeking 'someone with a sizable fortune and a substantial sense of humor to be the Benefactor of this program in which his or her family will compete game show style, to be

named the heir to a fortune'
(www.thewilltv.com/main.html cited by Andrejevic
2004). Andrejevic writes of other developments of the
'genre' in the USA. There is *Joe Millionaire* which seems
to be 'taking a swipe at the recent spate of marriage
reality formats that encourage women to compete for the
attentions of a wealthy bachelor (and in one case, for
men to compete for the attentions of an eligible
"bachelorette").' In *Joe Millionaire*, six women were sent
to France to compete with each other for the hand of an
'eligible millionaire – little did they know that he was
nothing other than a construction worker earning less
than $20,000 a year. If it is thought by anyone in the UK
that there is an excess of reality television programmes,
then have a look what is at the time of writing (2004) on
in the US. NBC is running at least 20 reality programmes
including *Who Wants to Marry My Dad?* which features
'adult children helping their single father find a mate'
(http://www.sirlinksalot.net/marrymydad.html) and *Fear
Factor*, described thus:

> *has six different contestants compete each week
> against each other and themselves in a series of
> challenges designed to confront individual fears
> and phobias. Stunt coordinators will assist the
> contestants in performing various dangerous
> and/or frightening activities, such as free-falling
> from a 12-story building with only a quarter-inch
> cable to stop their bodies from hitting the concrete
> pavement below. Matt Kunitz and John de Mol of
> Endemol USA are producing the series. According
> to NBC these stunts should not be attempted by
> anyone, anywhere, anytime.*
> **(http://www.sirlinksalot.net/fearfactor.html)**

As of spring 2004, there are more than 150 or more
reality shows on US TV: at 26, Fox has the most, and that
does not include the UK imports.

The Blaine Experience
In the autumn of 2003 reality TV 'crossed over' into reality – or was it the other way around? – when the American illusionist David Blaine was suspended from a crane near Tower Bridge in London. He hovered there for a month, highlighting the ancient pedigree of Reality TV: at one and the same time he incorporated elements of both 'performance art' and medieval street-spectacle. It was also a very lucrative piece of 'Reality TV', insofar that it was marketed as such worldwide. That, while it was happening, it was not broadcast as a television series hardly mattered – given the amount of TV time it was afforded on news and magazine programmes, it virtually functioned as such.

Blaine's 'performance' had all six key elements of a reality TV show:

- a fixed and closed location;
- time bound;
- an unusual task;
- an element of either endurance and/or competition;
- audience participation;
- broadcast live.

Scheduling Reality
Many (not all) reality shows have a distinctive scheduling pattern: they tend to be 'stripped' across several evenings over a given number of weeks. High profile shows, such as *Big Brother* or *I'm a Celebrity, Get Me Out of Here* are screened every evening. *I'm a Celebrity* ran for approximately 20 hours over a two week period in spring 2004, culminating with an audience of about 18 million for the final episode. Typically, they have an hour or 90 minutes during evening prime time with a follow up later in the evening. Key episodes are those where members of the 'cast' are voted off by the audience.

In June and July of 2004, UK *Big Brother* (the fifth series) was accorded what was by then its normal scheduling pattern, screening every evening, sometimes in two scheduled programmes. The attempt to gain a larger audience in the face of growing boredom with reality television was enriched with two tactics that were to provoke controversy. First the producers 'upped the ante' in the recruitment of the contestants. Always looking for 'interesting' people, on this occasion they deliberately set out to find some who would conflict with each other. One contestant was overtly homophobic and so a homosexual man was recruited. Another was hostile to asylum seekers and so, yes, they recruited one. The producers got more than they bargained (one hopes so at least): towards the end of June there was a full-scale brawl that led to the programme temporarily going off air and the police being brought in to investigate. Naturally enough, once news of this hit the headlines the audience ratings rocketed (maybe the producers did get what they bargained for after all). It was also evident that the producers wanted at least the potential for sexual activity (and allegedly quite early in the series they got it): at the outset there were two beds fewer than the number of contestants. Endemol claim they are engaged in a serious social experiment: yet their critics suggest that they are engaged in cynical exploitation to maximise ratings.

Reality TV and the 'active' audience

The claims made for reality TV game shows are the same as those made for confessional talk shows, that they democratise the medium and empower the audience. In support of this claim is the idea that participants gain access to television who would not otherwise so do, and audiences are able to take an active part by contributing to the deselection of the participants. This is, however, a fairly minimalist level of 'democratisation'. Programme makers determine the rules and select the participants. There have, however, been instances of rebellion.

In Denmark, all nine housemates mutinied in protest at the conditions under which they were being kept. After a party on the roof, they simply went home. The show had to close down for the day; only three were persuaded to return and only then on the condition that they could have weekly visits from their friends and family (Andrejevic 2004, p. 27). In this instance, the programme makers met with the democratic imperative in a quite unexpected way.

Reality Television and Documentary

The other strand of reality TV, documentary, has its roots in the 1950s with the BBC's *Living in the Past*. Produced by John Percival, a group of volunteers, who 'had to survive on available resources', were filmed for 12 months living as Iron Age settlers. *Living in the Past* is the antecedent of Channel Four's *The 1900 House*. In this series, volunteers had to live as closely as possible in the manner of 1900, according to the role that had been assigned, be it the head of the household or a humble servant. Conditions were replicated to the smallest detail, including the clothing worn, the food eaten and the routine followed in the house. While there was no overt competition there was an element of endurance: narrative interest lay in watching how twenty-first century people would adjust to life as lived at the beginning of the twentieth century. The formula was repeated in *The 1940s House* and *The Trench*, where a group of volunteers lived under front-line World War I conditions (minus the gunfire).

A successful variation of the form was *Spitfire Ace*. Screened by the BBC early in 2004, the programme had two interwoven strands. Four flyers from different backgrounds (two civilians, a RAF University Air Squadron cadet and a RAF pilot) competed for the opportunity to fly one of the few surviving spitfires and have the same amount of combat training as a 1940 trainee pilot. This was interwoven with a documentary of the actual battle. *Spitfire Ace* successfully utilised elements of reality TV and traditional documentary in a way that illuminated both. It is clear, that for good or ill, reality television is here to stay. The programme formats that are currently popular will doubtless evolve into others. Whatever becomes of these formats, it is clear that the techniques of reality television have become part of the standard lexicon of programme making.

Bu has the dramatic rise in reality TV programming finally stalled? At the time of writing (spring 2004) there is evidence that the television audience is tiring of the 'genre', or at least its ubiquitous presence in the schedules. According to Ofcom:

> *Apart from complaints about too many advertisements, the most common concerns in our audience survey were that there are too many reality shows and too many celebrity shows. These concerns were echoed by the participants in our qualitative research seminars, who held strong views about the increase in derivative formats on the main networks, and who complained that the broadcasters often underestimate their audience.*
> **(Ofcom Review of Public Service Television Broadcasting 2004, p. 55)**

Within weeks of this report being published, a new reality show from ITV1, *Trouble in Paradise*, had a ratings disaster on its first night, with an average audience of just 2.7 million (11.5% of the audience).

Interactive Television Technology (iTV)

Broadcasting has always had a measure of 'interactivity'. Robert Silvey writes how in the 1930s he started audience research at the BBC by asking listeners to submit comments and queries about programmes on a postcard – a simple device employed for decades by both radio and television in the UK and the USA. The technology for facilitating audience interactivity was slow in developing and did not develop beyond the telephone until the 1990s with digital technology. Audience 'interactivity' was, from the 1930s, mostly a matter of broadcasting a programme in front of an audience. This was easily done in both the USA and UK with what were then very popular big bands such as those of Bennie Goodman and Artie Shaw. From the programme makers' perspective, the point of interactivity is to offer a sense of greater engagement in the hope that that this would lead to a larger audience.

By the time television had established itself in the 1950s, after its wartime silence, both game shows and light entertainment variety shows were being broadcast with a live audience. Examples were *Opportunity Knocks* (1956–1977), and *Saturday Night at the London Palladium* (ATV: 1955–1967 and 1973–1974). *Opportunity Knocks* was the *Pop Idol* of its day, but on a much larger scale. It was a fully fledged variety programme hosted by Hughie Green. The performers were all amateurs hoping for a first step towards stardom. Over the years the show launched a number of careers including those of Little and Large, Freddie Starr, Tom O'Connor, Para Ayres, Lena Zavaroni, Frank Carson and Les Dawson. Each week's show concluded with a brief reprise of each act. The audience's applause was 'measured' by a 'Clapometer', a simple but highly televisual device that engendered a little drama as the pointer nudged towards the previous highest score (or not, as the case may be). But this was not the end of the matter, as just as important as the studio audience was the vote by the television audience at home, registered via a postcard. The winner returned the following week to compete among a fresh batch of contestants. The final of a series featured the winners of each programme.

The popularity of the show was due in no small measure to the way that Green interacted with both studio and home audiences. In the way the programme addressed both audiences, incorporating the domestic audience into its formal structure, it was innovative and certainly pointed the way for programmes that followed. Indeed, the only difference between digitally interactive programme today, such as something like *Pop Idol* or *I'm a Celebrity...* is cosmetic, based on the available technology. The nature and degree of interactivity have not altered: the audience today presses the red button on the remote rather than posting a card; one method happens to be quicker, but the nature of the relationship between audience and programme has not substantially altered. It raises the question as to what is meant by 'interactive television'.

Subsumed by the term 'interactive television' are a range of activities and services provided by digital and cable television. These range from the well established, such as shopping channels, to the relatively new such as interactive sports and game shows. Interactivity, like 'access', has been written of in terms of empowering the audience. As with access this 'empowerment' is very limited if not illusory. Certainly audiences, through digital services such as those provided by Sky, now have more control over how they watch a televised football match and users of interactive shopping services (whether they be on the Internet or cable/digital TV) are able to avoid a trip to the shops; viewers of *I'm a Celebrity...* do not have to wait a week to find out which of the 'celebrities' have been sent packing. The fundamental relationship between broadcaster and audience, that of producer–consumer, remains unchanged. Television can certainly he used in different ways. Time shifting by recording a programme to watch later has been extended through developments such as TiVo and Sky plus; using their digital remote control, viewers are able to access additional information about a programme while they are watching it, such as a documentary, where topics can be further explored. Viewers of Sky news can, up to a point, construct their own news bulletins: an electronic menu enables them to follow up in more detail news stories of their choice. These are trivial developments when compared with the promise proffered by advocates of iTV and the Internet (both set to become fully converged).

The vision held out by iTV is the effacement of the difference between producer and consumer/audience. Reality TV offers the opportunity for the 'ordinary' person to participate either as an 'actor' or to determine the outcome to a show, as in game shows such as Big Brother, by choosing which of the contestants goes and who stays. The hierarchy of the producer–audience relations, epitomised by the near global power of Hollywood, is seemingly subverted by programmes that are unscripted and 'performed' by amateurs. As one fan put it: '... I like the fact that it's real people – people I can identify with, instead of superstars and Olympians' (Andrejevic, 2004, p. 9). For those who aspire to celebrity status, 'it is not just that it increases the chances of an obscure outsider to make it big but that it allows everyone to gain greater participation in and control over the mediated version of reality in which they are immersed' (ibid., p. 5). For the stars themselves, reality TV such I'm a Celebrity... and Celebrity Big Brother has provided an opportunity for fading ones 'to launch a comeback, or at least to pay the bills' (Andrejevic 2004, p. 3).

Access to television and the Internet has been ascribed a politically progressive function: access is equated with democracy and empowerment. But access to reality TV is controlled access – participation is circumscribed, first by a selection process carried out by the programmes makers and then by the quest for ratings that will determine the longevity of the series. During a run of a series of the American *Big Brother*, the producers wanted to 'move' into the house a new and livelier ratings boosting character. In order to maximise the ratings potential of the move itself, they decided to offer any one of the then current residents a suitcase containing $20,000 to leave the house. None took what amounted to a blatant bribe. The offer was bumped up first to $30,000 and then $50,000 - no one succumbed. To quote one, 'For me it was a question of integrity: I didn't want to be bought; I didn't want to sell my soul' (ibid., p. 145). Even taking into account the seemingly large prizes, these shows are cheap to produce; they attract large audiences that in turn draw in substantial advertising revenues, especially where a show like *Big Brother* is franchised internationally.

In 2001 a study commissioned by American Demographics showed that 45% of all Americans watch reality TV and that a fifth of these regard themselves as 'die hard' fans - that amounts to 1 in 11 Americans. At the same time, these shows are being made at a fraction of the cost of other programmes. Even relatively expensive shows like Survivor 'are often more than a third less expensive than comparable programming... With shows like *Big Brother* in Europe, the payoff can be enormous: a top rated show with relatively low production costs that can serve as the basis of an international franchise' (Andrejevic 2004, p. ll). There is, then, 'a somewhat different and more cynical version of democratisation, one whereby producers can deploy the offer of participation as a means of enticing viewers to share in the production of a relatively inexpensive and profitable entertainment product' (ibid., p. 6).

Interactivity, of course, cuts both ways – just as we are using television, television is using us. Interactive television (iTV) has a 'return path', that is to say that information does not only flow from the broadcaster to the viewer, but also from the viewer to the broadcaster. We have already seen that this forms the basis of modern TV and radio audience measurement, where the system feeds back details of what is being watched, and indeed who is watching. Notwithstanding the apocalyptic tone of Spy TV, attention is drawn to the commercial nature of much of this technology that actually reinforces the rational producer–consumer relationship under the guise of 'empowering' the audience. David Burke outlines the various ways in which iTV, now and in the future, monitors audiences for commercial advantage. Every digital set-top box is identifiable through an individual IP address. Some have a 'store and hold' facility, which is a memory that can hold a viewer's data and then transmit it through domestic telephone lines. This data is used to build up a profile of the viewer that can be used as the basis for targeted advertising. There are dedicated consumer data analysis companies, 'some are huge data warehouses, some are small consulting firms that just do analysis. These companies have experience with direct marketing, and are now moving that experience into a world of faster turnaround, where cycles of offer, response and new offer will happen in a matter of hours instead of months' (David Burke: http://www.whitedot.org/issue/iss_story.asp?slug=shortS pyTV).

Thus iTV becomes a valuable commercial asset because of the information that can be fed back about a viewer's life style and tastes. In turn, individual homes can be targeted with appropriate advertisements and programmes. This works because with an iTV set, every 'click' of the remote control sends information to the database. A 'clickstream' for each television is created and is analysed, producing a profile that can be used to target consumers with direct marketing either directly through the television, telephone or post.

When TiVo was launched in 2000, Anthony Lewis wrote in the *New York Times*, describing it as being able to:

> *Accumulate, in atomic detail, a record of who watched what and when they watched it. Put the box in all 102 million American homes, and you get a pointillist portrait of the entire American television audience. .... Already TiVo and Replay know what each of their users does every second, though both companies make a point of saying that they don't actually dig into the data to find out what who did what, that they only use it in the aggregate. Whatever. They know.*
> **(cited in Andrejevic 2004, p. 23)**

There is nothing particularly sinister about any of this: for many of us it happens anyway, in supermarkets, for example, and almost every time we use the Internet, a 'cookie' will have encapsulated information about us. Anyone using a store card or self-scanning device is profiled with every visit. There is the view, however, that in the future all electrical appliances will be interconnected and even the simple act of opening the fridge and taking out a bottle will of milk could result in a 'click' that will send more information to a database.

Constant and detailed surveillance is the 'flip side' of increasingly convergent interactive technologies. It is, in part, the answer as to why if 'network technology is *inherently* revolutionary ...... bureaucratic, corporate, and financial elites are so enthusiastic about, and so heavily interested in the success of this technology' (Darin Barney cited in Andrejevic, 2004, p. 15). It is through surveillance that iTV and the Internet are economically exploited. Far from devolving control to the audience and opening up television to 'access', it has become a means through which commerce is able to create and maintain new markets. The individual customisation of mass produced products has a superficial lure, yet as Andrejevic argues, 'the promise of customisation or individuation might be a virtual one: customisation will take place to the extent that it conforms to the set of rules defined by producers' (ibid., p. 51). This applies equally to reality TV with its illusory promise of participation that digital technology seemingly offers.

Postscript: Positioning the Audience

To be a 'viewer', 'spectator' or in any other way an audience is to accede to a relationship over which we have some, but not full control. The only way in which total 'control' can be asserted is by denying that relationship and turning off, walking out of the room or closing the book. Through a set of institutional and textual practices the audience is 'positioned' into a text, that is 'invited' to take a particular point of view, to negotiate a narrative in a certain way and encouraged to accede to a given ideological position. The audience, however, is not compelled to go along with any of this – audiences will use a text as they choose and make what meanings they will. The positioning of an audience is not the same as its complete subjugation: communication is always a two way process even if the relations of power are not equitable.

'Audience position' can be understood in at least two different ways:

1. The way audiences relate to media institutions.
2. The way audiences are inscribed into 'reading positions' within texts.

Media institutions have a variety of ways of attracting and maintaining audiences through their positioning in relation to them. Texts of all kinds, films, television/radio programmes, books, newspapers, magazines are sold not only on the basis of what they are in themselves, but by the way the audience perceives the institutions that produce them. Institutions create a 'corporate image' that in some way accords to the way audiences see themselves. In this sense, the audience is as much 'inscribed' into a media institution as it is within a text. In both radio and television, each station/channel must build an image with which an audience can identify through the way it is marketed, but also through an institutional 'voice'. This 'voice' is constructed by, and articulated through:

- choice of programme content;
- the form of the programme;
- style of programme;
- style and manner of presenters;
- style and form of trailers;
- marketing.

In the case of cinema, the building itself will 'speak' to the audience through everything from its décor and furnishings to the refreshments on offer. One, or possibly the main, reason why there has been such a marked growth in cinema attendance since the 1980s has the been the multiplex. In fact the growth of cinema attendance in the UK runs more or less parallel with the increase in the number of multiplexes.

The Audience in the Text: The Spectator–Reader

This *Guide* has, thus far, largely concerned itself with theory only as far as it has born directly on approaches to researching actual audiences. There is, however, an important and very extensive body of work that takes as its subject of enquiry not a socially constituted 'real' audience (bearing in mind just how elusive that is) but a more abstract entity understood as 'a correlate of the institution of the cinema and a hypothetical point of address by filmic discourse' (Cook and Bernink 1999, p. 366). The symbolic figure that stands in for audience (reader/spectator) in this body of theory is the 'subject' as conceptualised by the psychoanalyst Jacques Lacan. Drawing on Ferdinand Saussure and structural linguistics, Lacan argues that the unconscious is a sign system that functions like a language. Inflecting the Freudian model of the unconscious, Lacan posits the individual 'self' not as a unified ego, but as something that is something far more fluid being 'consistently produced and transformed by the unconscious, which is itself produced through the language and perceptions of others' (Lacan, cited in Cook and Bernink 1999, p. 366).

The French philosopher, Louis Althusser, incorporated Lacan's ideas about language and the unconscious, along with Karl Marx's theory of alienation, into his theory of the subject. Althusser's theory begins with his re-working of Marx's economic base/superstructure model. For Althusser, the relationship between the two was less deterministic. He understood ideology as having a degree of relative autonomy in relation to the economic base, opening up spaces of resistance to the dominant ideology. The way that the state maintained authority over its constituent subjects was explained by Althusser in terms of two modes of power. One is largely physical: the Repressive State Apparatuses (RSA), which maintain order and authority through force and include the police and the military. The RSAs act through the other dimension of state authority, the Institutional State Apparatuses (ISA): these include church, the courts, schools, the media, etc., which maintain order through consent, largely through the reproduction and maintenance of the dominant ideology. It's with the ISAs that there is most obviously a degree of autonomy (although it is also the case with the RSAs). In both education and the media, for instance, work of all kinds will sometimes run counter to the dominant ideology. The ISAs, in constantly reproducing the dominant ideology, will 'hail' individuals and 'interpolate' them as certain kinds of subjects, summoning them to take up their appropriate role in society. This will happen in a myriad of ways, each individual constantly assuming different roles – mother, father, student, consumer, and so on. Althusser maintained that the process of interpolating individuals as social subjects is subtle and largely imperceptible, leading to the illusion that they are 'consistent, rational, and free agents'.

Cinema is also an ISA and in its mainstream forms works to reproduce the dominant ideology through the process of interpolation. Some film theorists have argued that Hollywood cinema in particular binds the spectator to dominant ideology through interpolation, a process that is masked by providing the individual with the illusory sense that s/he is 'a unified, transcendent, meaning making subject' (Cook and Bernick 1999, p. 366). Spectatorship was a dominant theme in 1970s film theory and followed two intersecting paths, apparatus theory and the analysis of textual systems.

Apparatus Theory

Apparatus theory conceptualises cinema as an institutional and ideological machine embracing the general conditions of cinematic spectatorship and the effects of these on the viewing subject. Jean-Louis Baudry (*Ideological Effects of the Cinematographic Apparatus*, 1970) argues that even the camera/projector lens is ideologically determined insofar as it reproduces the renaissance perspective that places the viewing subject at the originating point of vision, the source of the controlling gaze. The camera-projector ensures 'the setting up of the "subject" as the active centre and origin of meaning (Baudry 1970). In broader ideological terms, renaissance perspective represented a shift from a deistic to a more humanist view of the world, where 'man', if not displacing god, occupied more of the centre stage: it visually embodied the illusion of control, or in Lacanian psychoanalytic terms, the unified subject for whom meaning is both imminent and transparent. The illusion of the unified subject is embodied in the 'machine' of cinema itself, which positions the spectator 'as the transcendent vanishing point of filmic address... the spectator imagines himself or herself as a transcendent meaning making subject ' (Cook and Bernink 1999, p. 366). According to apparatus theory the spectator is deluded into thinking that s/he is an active maker rather than a passive recipient of meaning. This clearly 'flies in the face' of contemporary ethnographic approaches to audience research, which are predicated upon an active, meaning-making audience.

Overlapping with 1970s apparatus theory was a text-based theory of spectatorship. Informed by Lacan's theory of the subject, theorists such as Stephen Heath and Raymond Bellour undertook a very detailed analysis of films that seemed to represent the cinematic institution *par excellence* – Hollywood. Apparatus theory/textual systems have been criticised as being too mechanistic and, as with textual systems analysis, positing a passive spectator. Apparatus theory/textual systems attempt to understand the ways in which the institution of cinema has inscribes within it viewing positions which the viewer is asked to take up. However, apparatus theory/textual systems is regarded, by many critics, as being far too generalised, not taking into account crucial differentiating factors within an audience, such as race and gender. The best known early critique of apparatus theory/textual systems is Laura Mulvey's *Visual Pleasure in Narrative Cinema* (1975) in which she argues that the classic Hollywood film established the male star as the instigator of action while the female was subordinated to being the object of his, and that of the male spectator's, desire: the male controlled *the look* whilst the female was *looked at*. The paradox of the function of the female form in classic Hollywood is that at one and the same time it functions as the object of desire for the male gaze but in so doing freezes the flow of the narrative: the 'presence of woman is an indispensable element of spectacle in normal narrative film, yet her visual presence tends to work against the development of a story-line, to freeze the flow of action in moments of erotic contemplation' (Mulvey, 1975). Drawing on Lacan, Mulvey argued that although the female form was displayed for male pleasure (the male protagonist and male audience) it also represented a threat, invoking unconscious anxieties about sexual difference and castration. This could be dealt with by the male by subjecting the woman to his sadistic gaze and punishing her for being different, or difference could be denied by fetishising the female by overvaluing certain parts of her body such as her breasts or legs. The threatening, castrating female is usually punished at the end of the narrative, as in film noir where she is usually killed. Freud and Lacan argued that the castration complex was universal and was the originating, and perpetuating, cause of patriarchy. Mulvey sought to show that film in particular was part of patriarchal society's signifying practices that worked to reinforce myths about women as well as being a source of male pleasure. But, importantly, Mulvey did not regard this system as fixed and unchangeable as there was always the possibility of finding a new language of desire.

If classic Hollywood was predicated exclusively upon the male gaze, then the viewing position of the female spectator was highly problematic. One of the problems with Mulvey's essay, quickly identified by feminist critics, is that she leaves out any consideration of the female spectator. Mulvey's response to this criticism was *Afterthoughts on 'Visual Pleasure and Narrative Cinema'* (1981) which was inspired by King Vidor's *Duel in the Sun* (1946) in which she characterised the female spectator as unconsciously shifting between both an active masculine and passive feminine identity. Freud had argued that there was one libido which performs both masculine and feminine functions and 'there is a repeated alternation between periods in which femininity and masculinity gained the upper hand' (Freud 1905/1964, p. 251, cited by Mulvey, 1989, in Kaplan 1990, p. 25). Applying this to film, Mulvey concluded that a female spectator either identifies with the woman as object of the narrative or assumes a 'masculine' position, but this 'phantasy of masculinisation is always to some extent at cross-purposes with itself, restless in its transvestite clothes' (Mulvey 1981, p. 15).

Mulvey's work became a catalyst for a number of wide ranging articles and critiques, many of whom argued that Mulvey's approach was too reductive and that apparatus theory, whether or not it took into account issues of gender, was still part of a long established tradition whereby masculinity is the established norm, denying a place for women.

Richard Dyer (1986) and Steve Neale (1983), contra Mulvey wrote about the eroticisation of the male body in cinema. Mulvey had agued that the male body was not able to be sexually objectified in dominant 'Hollywood'. Dyer and Neale argued that this was not the case, that there were, albeit limited, circumstances in which this was possible, usually within the dramatic context of physical action that motivated bodily exposure (fighting, manual labour or other physical exertion) giving it narrative legitimacy over and above mere physical display. Other writers challenged the notion of the female as being merely the passive object in film. Drawing on psychoanalytic theories of women, such as those of Julia Kristeva, several feminists writers have argued that women 'could be represented as an active, terrifying fury, a powerfully abject figure, and a castrating monster' (Hill and Gibson 1998, p. 86). This view of women in film is far from the passive role traditionally ascribed to them.

Psychoanalysis exerted its greatest influence in film theory in the 1970s. It has since been criticised on a number of fronts:

1. The principal criticism has been its tendency to construct a passive viewer. Baudry's implied spectator was male and passive; Mulvey's male and active, but with a passive female.

2. It has also been attacked for being ahistorical: its focus on abstractions such as the Oedipus complex and

castration anxiety caused cine-psychoanalysis to be diverted from historical and political issues.

3. Its focus has been on an ideal, abstracted viewer rather an actual viewer. Spectatorship theory has tended not to consider differentiating factors in an audience such as race, age, sexual preference and social class. There does not seem to be any room either, for the possibility of resistance to a film's ideology, as is evident in the work on television carried out by researchers such as Morley and Jenkins.

4. A crucial criticism is that psychoanalysis is not a science and that its theories are not based upon 'hard' evidence and cannot by empirically verified. The response to this criticism is that the kind of theoretical abstraction with which cine-psychoanalysis engages cannot be empirically verified. Freudian-Lacanian psychoanalysis is predicated upon a non-linear relation between the conscious and the unconscious. Surface signs of mental and emotional phenomenon may have no clear connection with what is happening at an unconscious level, subject as it is to the various 'distortions' of displacement, repression and transformation. The relations between manifest phenomena and the unconscious can only be surmised through psychoanalytic reading.

Not withstanding the criticisms that have been levelled at it, psychoanalysis still has a role to play in the theorising of spectatorship. An interesting example is the work of Homi K. Bhabha who has drawn on psychoanalytic theory in his work on colonialism and post-colonialism. Work on racism in the cinema has tended to focus, for example, on stereotyping and narrative roles. Bhabha has written about the process of subjectification in terms of the representation of 'otherness' through the use of cinematic codes, shifting the terms of the debate about colonialism and racism from just 'image' (negative or otherwise) to the *filmic construction of relations of power*. A key work is his *The Other Question* (1992). Bhabha draws on Freud's theory of castration and fetishism in his analysis of stereotypes of black and white, arguing that they invoke in the colonial subject the fantasy of 'an ideal ego that is white and whole.' (Bhabha 1993, p. 322 cited in Hill and Gibson 1998, p. 88).

Other areas in which psychoanalysis has an important role are in queer and body theory. As with Bhabba, there is a rejection of praising 'positive' stereotypes and rejecting 'negative' ones - 'positive' images in film can be just as demeaning. The focus of 'queer theory' is to analyse the way desire is constructed and how cinematic pleasures are offered to an audience. Judith Butler (*Gender Trouble*, 1990) criticises the concept of fixed gender identities in psychoanalyses. This has been influential in work on the representation of gays and lesbians in film. 'Body theory' is concerned with representation of the body, especially (in the 1980s and 1990s) in the horror film. Much of this work has sought to make connections between the representation of the body – the monster – in film and the social, political and familial 'body'. It is clear from the scope of the work that draws on psychoanalysis that it still plays an important role in film theory. The difference between now and the 1970s is that it is no longer used as a monolithic: for many theorists it remains a useful tool among many.

Postscript

When on 19 August 1987 Michael Ryan went on the rampage through Hungerford, a quiet English market town, shooting dead 15 people and wounding 14 others with a 9mm semi-automatic before turning the gun on himself, it was quickly assumed by the tabloids that the catalyst for this tragedy had been Ryan's enthusiasm for the film *Rambo* (1985): he was dubbed 'Evil Rambo'. It was subsequently shown that, at best, this conclusion was tenuous. It seems that he owned neither television nor video and neither, as was claimed by the tabloids, was he dressed like the character played by Sylvester Stallone. This was not the only violent instance where there was a rush to judgement and film or television (or both) blamed. It turned out that what Ryan did possess, in large numbers, were magazines and books about guns and military matters. There were no demands that these books and magazines be banned. Why in this case, and others, is film/TV so readily cited as the causal culprit rather than books or magazines? It is not that these and other media have been the focus of concern at various times in the past – they have (and now we must add computer games to the list) – but television and film do seem to have a special place in the pantheon of villainy. The reason for this is the referential power of the photographic image. For André Bazin, film was 'the most realistic of the arts'.

The naturalistic nature of the photographic image has a particular force and it is this that arouses such fear and concern, especially when yoked to narrative. The dynamics of narrative are such that its photographic representation, through the manipulation of point-of-view, arouses in the spectator the state of mind often alluded to as the suspension of disbelief. It is a useful phrase as 'suspension' implies being recalled to the world of ordinary reality once the final credits have rolled and the lights have come back up – in fact we never really lose our grip with reality at all: the tease of cinema is that it enables us to enjoy the temporary illusion that we have done so.

In any ordinary sense of 'the audience', the media do not know to whom they are talking, other than in the broadest terms. Research might have told them that statistically, the typical audience member is this or that, possessing a cluster of characteristics that amount to the non-existent average. But that is all. Huntley writes of how some media organisations crystallised these broad feature into generally patronising and demeaning fictional characters. At the time he was writing, one independent radio station in the UK encouraged their presenters in training to 'get to know "Doreen"', a figure who had evolved over time as representing the typical listener. One is inclined to think that such inventions serve the function of encouraging the presenters to believe that they are talking to *someone*, whoever that may be, rather than no one at all. The reason for that is that both sides of a communication relationship need to know that is what they are in – a relationship. Even a solitary radio announcer – maybe *especially* a solitary radio announcer – needs to believe that s/he is talking to *someone*. That 'someone' will be incorporated into their mode of address, just as we all adjust the way speak – or even write – depending on who we are talking to. In that sense we are all like Woody Allen's Zelig, adjusting to whom we are communicating.

Bibliography

Abercrombie, Nicholas, *Television and Society*, Polity Press, 1996.

Abercrombie, Nicholas and Longhurst, Brian, *Audiences*, Sage Publications, 1998.

Alasuutari, Pertti (ed.), *Rethinking the Media Audience: The New Agenda*, Sage Publications, 1999.

Alasuutari, Pertti, *Researching Culture: Qualitative Method and Cultural Studies*, Sage Publications, 1995.

Andrejevic, Mark, *Reality TV: The Work of Being Watched*, Rowan and Littlefield Publishers, 2004.

Ang, Ien, *Watching Dallas*, Routledge, 1990.

Ang, Ien, *Desperately Seeking the Audience*, Routledge, 1991.

Ang, Ien, *Living Room Wars: Rethinking media audiences for a postmodern world Routledge*, 1996.

Aronson, Elliot, *Social Animal*, W.H.Freeman, 2003.

BBC, *The Public and the Programmes: A Report on an Audience Research Enquiry BBC*, 1959.

Bacon-Smith, Camille, *Enterprising Women*, University of Pennsylvania Press, 1992.

Ball-Rokeach, Sandra J. and Cantor, Muriel G. (eds) *Media, Audience, and Social Structure*, Sage Publications, 1986.

Barwise, Patrick and Ehrenberg *Television and its Audience*, Sage Publications, 1988.

Baudry, Jean-Louis, 'Ideological Effects of the Basic Cinematographic Apparatus', in *Film Theory and Criticism*, Mast, G. et al (eds), Oxford University Press, 1992.

Bazalgette, Cary and Buckingham, David, *In Front of the Children: Screen Entertainment and Young Audiences*, BFI, 1995.

Berman, Ronald, *How Television Sees its Audience*, Sage Publications, 1987.

Blau, Herbert, *The Audience*, The John Hopkins University Press, 1990.

Blumer, Jay G. and Katz, Elihu, *The Uses of Mass Communication: Current Perspectives on Gratification Research*, Sage Publications, 1974.

Bobo, Jacqueline, 'The Color Purple: Black Women as Cultural Readers', in *Female Spectators*, Pribham, D. (ed.), Verso, 1992.

Bogart, Leo, *Commercial Culture: Mass Media System and the Public Interest*, Oxford University Press, 1996.

Brooker, Will and Jermyn, Deborah, *The Audience Studies Reader*, Routledge, 2003.

Bower, Robert T., *The Changing Television Audience in America*, Columbia University Press, 1985.

Buckingham, David, *Public Secrets, Eastenders and its Audience*, BFI, 1987.

Buckingham, David (ed.), *Reading Audiences, Young People and the Media*, Manchester University Press, 1993.

Buckingham, David, *Moving Images: Understanding Children's Emotional Responses to Television*, Manchester University Press, 1996.

Buckingham, David, *Children's Television in Britain: History, Discourse and Policy* BFI, 1999.

Buckingham, David, (ed.) *Small Screens: Television for Children*, Leicester University Press, 2002.

Buckingham, David and Scanlon, Margaret, *Education, Entertainment and Learning in the Home*, Open University Press, 2003.

Buscombe, Edward, *British Television: A Reader*, Clarendon Press, 2000.

Butler, Jusith, *Gender Trouble*, Routledge, 1990.

Cantor, Muriel G, *The Hollywood TV Producer: His Work and His Audience*, Basic Books, 1971.

Cavender, Gray and Fishman, Mark (eds), *Entertaining Crime*, Aldine de Gruyter, 1998.

Cole, Barry and Oettinger, Mal, *Reluctant Regulators: the FCC and the Broadcast Audience*, Addison-Wesley, 1978.

Comstock, G. and Lindsey, G., *Television and Human Behaviour*, Rand, 1975.

Cook and Bernink, *The Cinema Book 2nd Edition*, London: BFI, 1999.

Cartmell, Deborah, Hunter, I.Q., Kaye, Heidi and Whelehan, Imelda, *Trash Aesthetics: Popular Culture and its Audience*, Pluto Press, 1997.

Cartmell, Deborah and Hunter, I.Q. and Whelehan, I., *Sisterhoods*, Pluto Press, 1998.

Corner ,John; Schlesinger, Philip and Silverstone, Roger *International Media Research*, Routledge, 1997.

Crissel, Andrew, *Understanding Radio*, Routledge, 1986, 1994.

Cumberbatch, Guy, *Media Violence: Science and common sense Psychology Review, Vol.1, No.2* April, 1977 pp2–6.

Cumberbatch, Guy et al, *The Portrayal of Violence on British Television*, Applied Psychology Division Aston University, 1987.

Cumberbatch, Guy and Howitt, Dennis, *A Measure of Uncertainty: the Effects of the Mass Media*, Broadcast Standards Council Research Monograph Series 1 John Libbey, 1989.

Cummings, Dolan, et al, *Reality TV: How Real is Real*, Institute of Ideas and Hodder and Stoughton, 2002.

Dickenson, Roger, Ramaswani Harindranath and Olga Linne, *Approaches to Audiences: A Reader*, Arnold, 1998.

Dorr, Aimee, *Television and Children: A Special Medium for a Special Audience*, Sage Publications, 1986.

Dorsch, T.S., *(trans.) Classical Literary Criticism*, Penguin Classics, 1965.

Dovey, Jon, *Feakshow: First Person Media and Factual Television*, Pluto Press, 2000.

Dyer, Richard, *Entertainment and Utopia*, Movie, No 24 Spring 1977.

Dyer, Richard, *Heavenly Bodies*, St. Martin's Press, 1986.

Ellis, John, *Seeing Things: Television in the Age of Uncertainty*, I.B. Tauris, 2000

Eaman, Ross A., *Channels of Influence: CBC Audience Research and the Canadian Public*, University of Toronto Press, 1994.

Ettema, James S. and Whitney, D. Charles, *AudienceMaking: How the Media Create the Audience*, Sage Publications, 1994.

Fishman, Mark and Cavender, Barry, *Entertaining Crime: Television Reality Progams*, Aldine de Gruyter, 1998.

Fiske, John, *Television Culture*, Methuen, 1988.

Fletcher, James E. (ed.), *Handbook of Radio and TV Broadcasting Research Procedures in Audience, Program and Revenues*, Von Nostrand Reinhold Company, 1981.

Fowles, Jib, *The Case for Television Violence*, Sage Publications, 1999.

Franklin, Bob, *British Television in the Age of Uncertainty*, Routledge, 2001.

The Gandhigram Institute of Rural Health and Family Planning *Exposure & Impact Analysis if Mass Media in Family Planning* (Audience Analysis),1980.

Greenberg, Bradley S. with Rampoldi-Hnilo, Lynn and Mastro, Dana *The Alphabet Soup of Television Program Ratings*, Hampton Press, Inc. N.J.

Goodhardt, G.J., Ehrenberg, A.S.C. and Collins, M.A., *The Television Audience*, Gower, 1987.

Gray, Ann, *Video Playtime: The Gendering of a Leisure Technology*, Routledge, 1992.

Gunter, B. and McClear, J., *Children and Television*, Routledge, 1997.

Hall, Stuart, 'Encoding/decoding the Television Discourse' (1974) in Centre for Contemporary Cultural Studies (ed.), *Culture, Media, Language: Working Papers in Cultural Studies 1972–1979*, Hutchinson, 1980.

Halloran, James, *The Effects of Television*, Panther 1970.

Hammersley, Martyn, *Reading Ethnographic Research*, Longman, 1991, 1998.

Handel, Leo A., *Hollywood Looks at its Audience: A Report of Film Audience Research*, The University of Illinois, 1950.

Hargrave, Andrea Millwoood, *Radio & Audience Attitudes*, Broadcasting Standards Council, 1994.

Hartley, John, Goulden, Holly and O'Sullivan, Tim, *Making Sense of the Media*, Comedia, 1985.

Hobson, Dorothy *Crossroads: The Drama of a Soap Opera*, Methuen, 1982.

Hodge, Bob and Tripp, David, *Children and Television,* Polity Press, 1986.

Howitt, Dennis and Cumberbatch, Guy, *Mass Media Violence and Society,* 1975.

Iser, Wolfgang, *The Act of Reading,* Routledge, 1978.

Jenkins, Henry, *Textual Poachers: Television Fans and Participant Culture,* Routledge, 1992.

Jenkins, Henry, McPerson, Tara and Shattuc, Jane, *Hop on Pop,* Duke University Press, 2002.

Jhaly, S. and Lewis, J., *Enlightened Racism: The Cosby Show, Audiences and the Myth of the American Dream,* Westview Press, 1992.

Katz, Eliku, Blumler, Jay and Gurevitch, Michael, *The Use of Mass Communication,* Sage, 1974.

Katz, Eliku and Lazarsfeld, Paul T., *Personal Influence,* The Free Press of Glencoe, 1955.

Kellner, Douglas, *Media Culture,* Routledge, 1995.

Lazarsfeld, Paul T., *The People's Choice,* Columbia University Press, 1965

Lazarsfeld, Paul T. and Stanton, Frank, *Radio Research,* Duell, Sloan and Pearce, 1941.

Lin, Carolyn A. and Atkin, David J. (eds) *Communication, Technology and Society: Audience Adoption and Uses,* Hampton Press, 2002.

Leavis, F.R., *Mass Civilisation and Minority Culture,* The Minority Press, Gordon Fraser at St.John's College, Cambridge, 1930.

Leavis, F.R. and Thompson, Denys, *Culture and Environment: the Training of Critical Awareness,* Chatto and Windus, 1933.

Lewis, L., *The Adoring Audience,* Routledge, 1992.

Livingstone, Sonia M., *Making Sense of Television: the Psychology of Audience Interpretation,* Pergamon Press, 1990, 1995.

Lull, James, *Inside Family Viewing: Ethnographic Research on Television's Audiences,* Routledge, 1990.

Lull, James and Hinerman, Stephen, *Media Scandals: Morality and Desire in the Popular Culture Marketplace,* Polity Press, 1997.

Maine, Basil, *The B.B.C. and its Audience,* Thomas Nelson and Sons, Ltd., 1939.

Mankiewicz, Frank and Swerdlow, Joel, *Remote Control: Television and the Manipulation of American Life*, Times Books, 1978.

Market Information Services Ltd., *The Size and Nature of the Poster Audience*, Mills and Rockleys, 1949.

Mayne, Judith *Cinema and Spectatorship*, Routledge, 1993.

McQuail, Denis, *Audience Analysis*, Sage Publications, 1997.

McQuail, Denis *McQuail's Reader in Mass Communication Theory*, Sage Publications, 2002.

McQuail, Denis and Windahl, Sven, *Communication Models for the Study of Mass Communication*, Longman, 1981.

McQuail, et al, 'The Television Audience – a revised perspective' in McQuail, Dennis (ed.) *Sociology of Mass Communications*, Penguin, 1972.

Miller, William L., *Media and Voters: The Audience, Content, and Influence of Press and Television at the 1987 General Election*, Clarendon Press, 1991.

Morley, David, *The Nationwide Audience*, BFI, 1980.

Morley, David, *Family Television: Cultural Power and Domestic Leisure*, Comedia Publishing Group.

Morley, David and Brunsdon, Charlotte, *The Nationwide Television Studies*, Routledge, 1999.

Mullan, Bob, *Consuming Television: Television and its Audience*, Blackwell, 1997.

Mulvey, Laura, 'Visual and Narrative Pleasure', 1975, in *Visual and Other Pleasures*, Macmillan, 1989.

Mytton, Graham, *Handbook on Radio and Television Audience Research*, BBC World Service Training Trust, 1999.

Neale, Steve, 'Masculinity in Sport', *Screen* 24 (6), 1983.

Noh, Eun-Ju, *Metarepresentation: A Relevance Theory Approach*, John Benjamins Publishing Company, 2000.

Nueman, W. Russell, *The Future of the Mass Audience*, Cambridge University Press, 1991.

Nightingale, Virginia, *Studying Audiences: The Shock of the Real*, Routledge, 1996.

Oswell, David, *Television, Childhood and the Home: A History of the Making of the Child Television Audience in Britain*, Clarendon Press, 2002.

Palmer, Patricia, *The Lively Audience: A Study of Children Around the TV Set*, Allen & Unwin, 1986.

Pilkington, Adrian, *Poetic Effects: A Relevance Theory Perspective*, John Benjamins Publishing Company, 2000.

Radway, Janice A., *Reading the Romance: Women, Patriarchy and Popular Literature*, University of North Carolina Press, 1991.

Radway, Janice A., 'Reception Study: Ethnography and the Problems of Dispersed Audiences and Nomadic Subjects', in *Cultural Studies 2*, 3:29–39, 1988.

Remckstorf, Karsten and McQuail, Dennis, *Media Use as Social Action: A European Approach to Audience Studies*, John Libbey, 1996.

Rouchota, Villy and Jucker, Andreas, H. (eds), *Current Issues in Relevance Theory*, John Benjamins Publishing Company, 1998.

The Screen Advertising Association, *The Cinema Audience: A National Survey*, 1960.

Seiter, Ellen, Borchers, Hans, Kreutzner and Warth, Eve-Marie, *Remote Control*, Routledge, 1989.

Sheppard, D., *Audience Reactions to a Television Feature Programme on Road Accidents*, Transport and Road Research Laboratory, 1982.

Silverstone, Roger and Hirsch, Erich (eds) *Consuming Technologies: Media and Information in Domestic Spaces*, Routledge, 1992.

Silverstone, Roger, *Television and Everyday Life*, Routledge, 1994.

Silvey, Robert, *Who's Listening? The Story of BBC Audience Research*, Allen & Unwin, 1974.

Smith, Anthony *The Shadow in the Cave: the Broadcaster, The Audience and the State*, Quartet Books, 1976.

Sobchack, Vivian *The Addressee of the Eye: A Phenomenology of Film Experience*, Princeton University Press, 1992.

Staiger, Janet *Interpreting Films: Studies in the Historical Reception of American Cinema*, Princeton University Press, 1992.

Steiner, Gary A., *The People Look at Television: A Study of Audience Attitudes*, Alfred A. Knopf, 1963.

Stokes, Melvyn and Maltby, Richard, *Hollywood Spectatorship: Changing Perceptions of Cinema Audiences*, BFI, 2001.

Suleiman, Susan R. and Crosman, Inge (eds), *The Reader in the Text*, Princeton University Press, 1980.

Svennevig, Michael, *Television Across the Years: The British Public's View*, ITC, 1998.

Taylor, Greg, *Artists in the Audience: Cults, Camp and American Film Criticism*, Princeton University Press, 1999.

Television Bureau of Advertising *Report on Audience Composition*, How to Reach, 1959.

Tulluch, John and Jenkins, Henry, *Science Fiction Audiences: Watching Doctor Who and Star Trek*, Routledge, 1995.

Ward, J.C., *Children and Television* An inquiry made by the Social Survey in October 1948 for a Departmental, Committee appointed by the Home Secretary, the Secretary of State for Scotland and the Minister of Education, Central Office of Information NS. 131, April 1949.

Webster, James G., Phalem, Patricia and Lichty, Lawrence W., *Ratings Analysis: The Theory and Practice of Audience Research*, Lawrence Erlbaum Associates, 2000.

Webster, James and Phalem, Patricia, *Mass Audience: Rediscovering the Dominant Model*, Lawrence Erlbaum Associates, 1997.

Williams, Raymond, *Television: Technology and Cultural Form*, Wesleyan University Press, 1974.

Zoonen, Liesbet van, *Feminist Media Studies*, Sage Publications, 1994.